LettsGuide

Denmark

Harold Dennis-Jones

First published 1975
by Charles Letts and Company Limited
Diary House, Borough Road, London SE1 1DW
Revised 1977, 1979, 1980, 1981
Designed and illustrated by Ed Perera
Cover: **Old Farm House, Nr. Ronde,** Jutland,
photograph: J Allan Cash Limited
Photographs: Danish Tourist Board, (pp 42, 44, 46, 52, 57, 60, 63, 77)
National Travel Association of Denmark, (p 48)
Harold Dennis-Jones, (pp 50, 56)

Printed in Great Britain by
Charles Letts (Scotland) Limited

Charles Letts & Co Ltd
London, Edinburgh, München & New York

Contents

What this book is all about

Denmark is a fascinating and lovely land. Yet it is still relatively little known to travellers. Lots of people, never having cycled through Denmark, even imagine that it is all completely flat. The countryside in fact is astonishingly varied; villages, towns, farmhouses, old churches, and manor houses and palaces are colourful and charming. Communications are excellent, and the enterprising, efficient, tremendously hospitable Danes have ways of doing things that we can all enjoy and learn from.

This little book sets out to do three main things. It tries to tell you enough about what you can see and do in Denmark and about the people you will meet there to enable you to decide where you want to go and what you want to do. It gives you an outline of how to travel to and in Denmark, so that you can decide your own routes. And it indicates costs sufficiently clearly to allow you to budget your visit accurately enough.

The book does not go lengthily into detailed accounts of what you ought to do and what you ought to see and how much exactly each item will cost.

Sensible travellers make up their own minds – and, anyway, finding the final details out for yourself and making your own choices constitutes one of travel's major excitements.

But if time and money is limited, as it is for nearly everyone, you will need guidance. That is what we aim to give. And wherever possible we try to tell you where you can get more up-to-date and fuller information both before you go and after your arrival. This applies specially, of course, to prices, which change continuously nowadays.

We would like to think that everything in this book is perfect. But we know there will be mistakes because we ourselves are anything but perfect. If you find any errors, be kind. Please write and tell us about them, so that at least we can avoid misleading future readers.

Have a good trip!

This volume deals with Denmark. A companion Letts Guide describes Norway and Sweden.

Facts at your fingertips

Travel preparations

Travel documents

To enter Denmark for up to three months (including time spent in other Scandinavian countries), British citizens need either a full passport or the British visitor's passport obtainable quickly at all principal post offices. Americans and Canadians need a passport. All necessary information, including passport application forms, can be obtained at post offices in all three countries. Various formalities (birth certificate or previous passport or other proof of identity, certified passport-size photographs, etc) are necessary, so begin the enquiry/application process well ahead of travel dates – several months if possible for full passports. In the USA first-time-ever applications involve a personal appearance before one of a wide range of specified officials. Most travel agents will help and advise.

In the UK and USA, but not in Canada, a wife can be included on her husband's passport and vice versa. In all three countries children under 16 can be included on a parent's passport. In such cases the passport cannot be used in the holder's absence.

Health

There are no compulsory vaccinations. But check that your polio and tetanus protection is up-to-date. Your doctor and certain UK authorised centres (consult the DHSS) will do whatever vaccinations you wish. Thomas Cook's Vaccination Centre in London gives also well-informed and up-to-date specialist advice.

Take a supply of any medicaments you use regularly adequate to last your stay (they will not necessarily be available in Denmark). Take also sun lotion to deal with strong sun if you are not regularly used to it, an antiseptic cream and a little plaster for small open wounds, aspirin or something similar for headaches, and anti-motion sickness pills if you suffer that way.

Insurance

Travel mishaps are thankfully scarce, but can be unbelievably expensive when they do occur. All travellers should insure themselves against loss of deposits paid to airlines, tour operators, hotels, and the like through their own or a near relative's illness or death in the family, etc. They need also insurance against the sometimes huge costs of special air tickets home for themselves and perhaps a companion, extra hotel costs, etc, following accident or illness abroad.

Every visitor to Denmark is entitled to free hospital in-treatment following an accident or sudden illness. UK-employed persons and pensioners and their families also receive substantial and rapid refunds of non-hospital doctors', dentists', and chemists' bills after paying them. Self- or non-employed get smaller refunds. US and Canadian residents pay for everything, and should make certain they have appropriate cover. Insurance for loss or theft of baggage or cash is also advisable for everyone. This sounds grim but insurance costs little.

In Britain many tour operators and most insurance companies have standard 'travel policies'. The AA, RAC, Caravan Club, and Camping Club of Great Britain arrange cover for members. Europ Assistance provides special medical and other help including an advice centre in London that never closes (phone or use the hotel telex), has air and road ambulances with qualified attendants constantly available to bring you home in serious cases, and maintains on-the-spot agents who not only help and advise but also guarantee payments without your having to find possibly large sums of ready cash. Europ Assistance is closely linked with similar organisations in most west European countries, and a related company provides non-medical insurance cover. But shop around and find a policy that suits your particular needs.

US and Canadian citizens should consult their travel agents and insurance companies or agents about any travel insurance they need. In Canada Ontario Blue Cross provides short-term foreign medical cover, and Voyageur Travel Insurance looks after everything. In the States CIEE and other organisations look after students. IAMAT (International Association for Medical Assistance to Travellers) issues lists of English-speaking doctors familiar with North American medical practice in return for a small membership fee. The World Medical Association gives similar help. The US Consumers' Union publishes a traveller's health guide.

Money
The easiest way of carrying money is in the form of traveller's cheques, obtainable from banks (not necessarily your own) and travel-banking firms such as the universally known Thomas Cook or American Express. Visa cheques, issued by a worldwide consortium of banks, are also widely known. Traveller's cheques are useful because they can be cashed almost anywhere, are accepted by many hotels, shops, airlines, etc, can often be refunded on the spot if lost (check this when buying them), and are not easily used by other people if stolen. In the UK buy them for preference from the 'High Street' banks, in the USA from Bank of America, Citibank, or Perera, and in Canada from the Bank of Montréal, the Canadian Imperial Bank of Commerce, etc. Apart from Thomas

Cook, American Express, and Visa, of course. At times of severe currency fluctuation it is always possible to buy cheques in a stable currency – Swiss francs, say, or Dutch florins, or West German marks. Major international credit cards like Diners, Visa, American Express, Master Charge, Carte Blanche, etc can be used to buy airline tickets, car hire, accommodation, meals, and maybe goods (mostly in more expensive establishments), and are especially useful in emergencies.

UK residents holding Visa or Eurocheque cards can cash up to two personal-account cheques (on any one day), each for up to £50, in European banks displaying Visa and Eurocheque signs respectively. Holders of other bank cards can usually do the same, but should enquire from their own banks where their cards are honoured. American Express cardholders outside their country of residence can obtain up to US$1000-worth of local currency against personal-account cheques in any period of 21 days.

Residents and visitors alike can bring as much money into the UK and take as much out as they wish, whether in banknotes, traveller's cheques, or any other form.

Package tours

In a country which you do not know a package tour is an attractive proposition. Packages nowadays need not by any means involve your being constantly shepherded around or dumped in a single large hotel with a large group. Coach tours through more than one European country are still admittedly popular. But more and more tours are nowadays deliberately designed to give you as much individual freedom and choice as possible. Yet all offer one dominating advantage – you make a single payment and leave someone else to bother about virtually all the practical chores like travel and hotel bookings, transfers, etc.

From Britain the number of companies offering inclusive packages is expanding steadily. While many concentrate on the week or weekend in Copenhagen, with travel by air, you can also take your choice of coach tours, cruises with calls at Danish and other ports, camping tours that include Denmark, sailing, canoeing, cycling, stays in farmhouses or in self-catering accommodation, and a lot else. DFDS Travel offer what is probably the widest selection, and at very reasonable prices. Other major operators include Scantours, Thomas Cook, Global, Cosmos, etc. Fly-drive holidays are available through British Airways and other companies. But many of the more specialised holidays are provided by smaller firms, not necessarily based in London. If your travel agent cannot find what suits you, consult the Danish NTO in London – though it must be admitted that many British travel firms, however well designed their products, seem singularly inept at telling people about them.

In North America Bennett Tours, Travellers (selling SAS Viking Holidays), Scanworld, Top of Europe Tours, and Wings are among the leading specialists. But Maupintour, Olson, Globus-Gateway, American Express, Thomas Cook, and many others include Denmark in their programmes. In Canada, P. Lawson Travel and Pedersen World Tours (both of Toronto) and Nordic Tours (Vancouver) are well worth considering.

More information

Even at this stage you will be wanting more information than can possibly be crammed into any book. *In Britain* your best sources are a good local travel agent, who will tell you about package tours and travel routes and possibly also about specialist holidays, and the Danish Tourist Board (National Tourist Office) in London. The latter have a very high reputation for coping promptly and effectively with even the most abstruse queries, including those that go outside the strict tourist sphere.

In the USA and Canada talk first to your travel agent, then if necessary write or call your nearest Danish or Scandinavian tourist office. (In some cases the countries operate combined tourist offices. See Addresses). Airlines operating to Denmark, especially SAS, are also knowledgeable. So are the specialist tour operators. Cultural and professional queries, however, are usually best dealt with through the Royal Danish Embassy.

Bookings

However you decide to travel (except on special student tickets) there can be solid advantages in making as many bookings as possible through a local travel agent. It costs nothing, uses an expert's knowledge (if you choose your agent carefully), and saves time and trouble. If difficulties arise over changed arrangements or the like the travel agent can advise and usually also help. In the USA and Canada most agents are capable also – for a fee – of designing itineraries, booking hotels, and so on for fully independent tours. In Britain, with a few exceptions, only firms handling business travel expect to do this.

Climate and clothes

Denmark has mostly mild winters and temperate summers. Summer lasts from June till the end of August. Weather at this period is changeable, but includes long, warm, dry periods. Day temperatures range from 18 to 25°C (64-77°F). It stays light far into the night and the few hours of darkness often seem chilly. Spring comes suddenly and is sometimes warm as well as delightful to see. Autumn brings a mass of colours, especially in the beech woods found in many parts of the country. May and September are the transitional months. Winters sometimes bring snow and ice – but everything and everywhere is kept so warm indoors that you need only heavy outerwear, not thick suits or dresses.

Formal clothes are needed in Denmark only for business meetings and when staying in top-grade hotels, where most people wear lounge suts and formal dresses for dinner. In summer, take woollies or something warm in case the weather turns cool, and a raincoat.

Getting to Denmark – and back

From Britain you can travel to Denmark by air or by sea, with rail links to and from the main ferry crossings. Through rail connections are also available for the shorter Dover-Ostend and Harwich-Ostend North Sea crossings.

From North America air travel is the only real possibility, though Royal Viking Line normally give one opportunity a year for one-way sea travel from New York to Copenhagen aboard a round-the-world cruise liner.

Air travel
From Britain British Airways and SAS (Scandinavian Air Services, the national airline of Denmark, Norway, and Sweden) both fly at least once and up to four times a day from London-Heathrow, London-Gatwick, Manchester, and Glasgow to Copenhagen. In addition, British Airways operate three services a week between Birmingham and Copenhagen. SAS link London-Gatwick and Århus daily except on Saturdays. Icelandic fly between Glasgow-Prestwick and Copenhagen. Aeroflot and Varig (the Brazilian airline) each have one service a week from Heathrow.

Tickets available include full-rate 1st- and economy-class returns valid for up to a year, one-month economy-class 'excursion' returns, and APEX fares permitting stays of up to three months. These last have to be bought and paid for a full month in advance. They permit of no alterations or stopovers, and refunds, should you have to cancel your trip, are restricted. For this reason buy insurance before paying for your ticket (or at the same time) to cover possible cancellation loss through such mishaps as your own or a family member's illness.

You can sometimes travel even more cheaply by buying what is legally a package tour using a charter flight or charter booking. Accommodation of some sort is obligatorily included in the price. But you are not obliged to use it. Tickets of this sort are known in the travel trade as 'minimum-rated packages'. Firms offering them include Cosmos, Falcon, Slade, Thomson, Travel Time, etc. To find what suits you best you need the help of an able and willing travel agent – able because a good deal of detailed knowledge is involved, and willing because selling you a cheap-rate ticket brings less commission than arranging a seat on a scheduled service.

From the USA SAS fly direct to Copenhagen from Anchorage, Los Angeles, Seattle, Chicago, and New York, and Northwest Orient from Minneapolis, Chicago, and New York. Finnair also operate one flight a week from New York to Copenhagen.

The fares you can pay range from full-rate 1st- and economy-class, with round-trip tickets valid for up to a year's stay, to economy-class 'excursion' round trips valid for stays of 14 to 45 days, cheaper APEX tickets involving various restrictions, and even cheaper 'mini-fares' which you also have to book 21 days in advance. Public charters are also available from New York and occasionally elsewhere. Travel agents and tour operators can use special GIT rates for groups (which they make up: you do not have to bother). Cheap one-way advance-purchase tickets allow people visiting several European countries to combine this leg of the journey with a cheap flight home from some other European gateway. It is virtually essential to get advice from a good travel agent.

From Canada SAS fly direct from Montreal and Air Canada from Toronto. Apart from some charters and special fares which can be used by travel firms booking groups you can choose between 1st- and economy-class travel for stays of up to a year and cheaper APEX round trips valid for stays of from 7 to 60 days. Special 'youth fares' are available to those aged 12-22 who are making long stays abroad. Again, consult your travel agent.

By sea
From Britain DFDS Danish Seaways sail all year daily from Harwich to Esbjerg, and 2-3 times a week from Newcastle to Esbjerg.

From North America As already mentioned, Royal Viking Line usually provide one chance a year to sail direct from New York to Copenhagen.

From continental Europe Some 28 ferry routes link Copenhagen and other Danish ports to Norway, Sweden, Finland, Poland, East Germany, and West Germany, often at very low prices. Consult any Danish or Scandinavian tourist office.

By rail
From Britain Special boat trains from London connect with all Danish Seaways' sailings from Harwich. A connection from Manchester serves night departures, and special trains run from Esbjerg quayside to Copenhagen, with connections to all other main towns in Denmark. Through connections are also provided between

London and Copenhagen via certain Dover-Ostend and Harwich-Hook of Holland crossings. Details are available from British Rail's Continental HQ and from all BR travel centres in UK and Britrail offices in North America.

Any UK resident over official retirement age holding the more expensive type of Senior Citizen Railcard can travel half-price on sections of a rail journey through the UK and in Holland, and get a reduction of 30% on Sealink/Seapseed services and in West Germany.

From the rest of Europe Numerous fast trains from every part of Europe, east as well as west, connect with the ferry routes to Denmark from neighbouring countries. And, with ten or more expresses a day linking Hamburg and Copenhagen, any train to Hamburg will connect with a Copenhagen departure.

Rail bargains Special-rate tickets make rail travel to and in Denmark economical and attractive. An InterRail card entitles UK residents aged up to 22 a month's half-rate travel in UK and Eire, half-fare on Sealink ferries, and free travel in 18 other countries including Denmark. North American residents of any age can buy a 1st-class Eurailpass providing unlimited rail travel for varying periods in 13 European countries, together with reductions on certain non-rail services. Alternatively, those aged up to 26 can buy in USA or Canada a Eurail Youthpass giving unlimited 2nd-class rail travel for two months in the same 13 countries and with the same additional reductions. InterRail tickets are bought from BR in the UK, Eurailpass and Eurail Youthpass from Britrail or any European railway office and many agencies in the USA and Canada.

Coach travel
From Britain Magic Bus provides cheap rides between London and Copenhagen via the Dover-Zeebrugge crossing, Belgium, Holland and West Germany. They drive non-stop. The journey can also be made less hurriedly by Europabus.

From the rest of Europe Europabus provides connections from most parts of Western Europe.

Customs
What you can take into Denmark All visitors can take into Denmark, without paying customs duty, everything intended for bona fide personal use, such as clothing, jewellery, cameras, musical instruments, portable typewriter, radio, and tape recorder, and sports equipment including boats (whether entering by sea or by road).

In addition, UK residents can bring in duty-free for personal use

1 litre of spirits (liquor) *or* 2 litres of dessert or fortified wine such as sherry; 2 litres of table wine; 200 cigarettes *or* 100 cigarillos *or* 50 cigars *or* 250 gr of smoking tobacco; 50 gr of perfume and $\frac{1}{4}$ litre toilet water; 500 gr of coffee *or* 200 gr of coffee extract; 100 gr of tea or 40 gr of tea extract; 2 kg sugar; and other gifts and souvenirs to a total value of 300 kr. If you are not in transit and are staying less than 24 hours (on a mini-trip to Esbjerg, for instance) you are allowed no spirits (2 litres of beer instead) and your tobacco is cut to 40 cigarettes or their equivalent. Only those over 17 are allowed duty-free alcohol and tobacco. To import duty-free coffee you have to be over 15.

If resident in Europe and coming direct from an EEC (Common Market) country such as Britain or West Germany you can add 50% to the above allowances and increase the gift-souvenir value to 1275 kr (no single item over 950 kr), provided the goods have been bought in ordinary shops and ordinary tax and duty paid. Your tobacco allowance is doubled if you are resident outside Europe and alcohol and other goods raised by 50% if you arrive from an EEC country.

What you can bring back On their return, UK residents over 17 may import duty-free purchases of 1 litre of strong spirits *or* 2 litres of fortified or sparkling wine, and an additional 2 litres of still table wine; and 200 cigarettes *or* 100 cigarillos *or* 50 cigars *or* 250 gr tobacco. Whatever their age they may also import 50 gr of perfume *and* $\frac{1}{4}$ litre toilet water, and £10 worth of gifts. Gifts are increased to £50 and other items by 50% if they were purchased in ordinary shops and normal tax paid in an EEC country such as France or Belgium (eg if you drive back), provided you return direct from that country. In case of doubt or difficulty consult the Customs' London HQ.

On returning to the USA you can import, without paying duty, bona fide gifts to a value of $300, provided you have not done this within the previous six months. If you are over 21 *and your gateway State allows* (check beforehand) you can bring in 1 US quart (.946 litre) of alcoholic drink (wine, beer, or liquor regardless of alcohol content). 200 cigarettes or 50 cigars or 3 lb of smoking tobacco, or proportional quantities, also come in duty-free. In addition, while abroad you can mail bona fide gifts other than tobacco or alcoholic drink to a value of $25 each, provided you label each present 'Unsolicited gift'. In case of doubt or difficulty you are advised to consult your Customs HQ

If you are returning to Canada After seven days or more abroad Canadian residents of any age, even babies, may import gifts worth CA$150, together with 50 cigars, 200 cigarettes, and 2 lb tobacco. They may also mail personal gifts, each under $15 in value (mark covers 'Unsolicited gift – value under $15'). Those above the age fixed by their gateway province, usually 18 or 19, may also import without paying duty 40 fl oz of wine or liquor or 24 pints of beer. For fuller details ask at your departure airport or quay for the Canada Customs brochure 'I Declare . . .': also for the booklet of advice to travellers 'Bon Voyage But . . .'. In case of doubt or difficulty about what you may be charged duty on, consult a Canadian Customs office.

When you are in Denmark

Getting around

You can travel about inside Denmark by air, sea, rail, bus, taxi, hire car or bike, and in some places by canoe.

Air travel Copenhagen's Kastrup Airport has regular connections to nine destinations in Jutland, to Odense on Fyn (Funen) island, and Rønne on Bornholm. Fares are reasonable, and reductions are available for families (two or more people), groups, children and young people, and everyone over 65. 'Green Fares' available on specified off-peak flights cost only half normal rates. With certain international tickets from UK and North America your onward flight to Odense and Jutland (but not to Bornholm) is free if requested when you make your bookings, provided you do not stop over in Copenhagen. SAS, other airlines operating to Denmark, and travel agents can give you details.

Rail travel Danish State Railways (DSB for short), helped by a few privately-owned outlying lines, maintain very efficient rail services throughout the country. Rail routes are supplemented by ferries and buses, many owned and operated by DSB, so that you can get from anywhere to anywhere quite quickly and without trouble.

Trains are comfortable, and extremely well heated in winter. Since distances are relatively short, neither sleeping accommodation nor dining cars are provided except on international trains. However, snacks and drinks can always be bought from mobile trolleys on major trains and on inter-city trains there are couchettes at night. Longer-distance journeys always involve transferring to a ferry at some point. This opportunity for a slap-up meal is avidly seized by all Danes, so be prepared for an uninhibited scramble as soon as the train starts to slow down. Expresses go bodily aboard ship at the Great Belt crossing, permitting everyone to dash for the restaurant unencumbered by baggage.

Specially fast trains are called *Lyntog* (Lightning Train), and the regular expresses *Intercity*. Seat reservations are obligatory on all trains crossing the Great Belt.

Reduced-rate tickets are available to families and all groups of two or more for all journeys, and to everyone over 65 for roundtrips. Children under four travel free: those between four and 12 are charged half price. Special circular tour tickets, permitting unlimited stopovers are also available for travel in Norway, Sweden, and Finland as well as Denmark. In the UK you can buy *Take Five* tickets permitting unlimited travel on any five days within a period of a month. For other rail bargains see Getting to Denmark – and back, above.

Buses and coaches The only long-distance coach services in Denmark are a few using the Zealand-North Jutland ferry routes. Extensive local service networks, however, radiate from all main and many minor towns. Central bus stations are usually alongside or very close to railway stations, and timetables are planned to make train-bus connections easy. Through tickets, covering rail and bus, can be bought at railway stations. Where trains and buses cover the same route tickets are interchangeable. Except in a few rare cases road travel tickets can also be bought on buses. Fares are as for 2nd-class rail.

Boat Though many of Denmark's islands are connected by bridges, well over 30 car-and-passenger ferries operate wholly inside the country, apart from the even more numerous international links. In addition, a few ferries are reserved wholly for passengers and bikes. Tickets can be bought on the quayside or on board. Passengers without cars, or with bikes or motorcycles, do not need advance reservations. Leaflets giving details of all main services can be obtained from Danish (or Scandinavian) tourist offices in the UK and North America, and from local tourist information offices in Denmark. See also Motoring.

Taxis are readily available throughout Denmark. Most drivers speak at least adequate English. In towns, taxis available for hire display signs saying *FRI*, but it may be easier to go to a cab rank (eg, at the railway station) or to telephone (you can use English). The Copenhagen taxi numbers are 35 35 35 and 35 14 20. Most taxis are fitted with meters which show the total price to be paid, including MOMS (turnover tax or VAT) and tip. If the taxi has no meter add 15% as tip. Do *not* attempt to do this for metered rides. Drivers dislike it.

Hire cars Anyone aged more than 20-25 (firms' arrangements vary) who holds a full (not provisional) state or national driving licence can hire a car without difficulty. Major international hire firms, such as Avis, Carop, Hertz, InterRent, etc, are represented in Denmark, and there are many local firms. You can make bookings in advance through an international agency or an airline or, in the

13

USA, a company specialising in European car rental. There are usually no drop-off charges provided you leave the car inside Scandinavia. Deposits are required unless you use a credit card accepted by the hirer. Check insurance details and buy additional collision insurance if needed. Lists of hirers inside Denmark are available from local tourist information offices.

Bikes can be hired in most towns and tourist areas at very reasonable rates. A deposit and proof of identity are needed before you take over the bike. Danish Railways also hire bikes from a number of stations from 1 April to 31 October.

Denmark is a cyclists' paradise, much appreciated by the Danes themselves. Special cycle tracks, marked CYKELSTI, are provided in picturesque parts of the country and also in towns such as Copenhagen, where you can ride to and from many suburbs almost without encountering other road traffic. Pre-booked cycle tours, which you start on any day you wish, are organised by provincial tourist offices, with accommodation either in hotels or in youth hostels. Bikes are carried free on country buses and very cheaply on trains. Detailed information is available from Danish (or Scandinavian) tourist offices outside Denmark as well as locally. See also Motoring.

Canoeing is a popular Danish sport, practised on many rivers and especially on the rivers and lakes in the lovely Silkeborg region. Numerous firms in this area hire canoes and camping equipment. Some very pleasant motor-launch excursions can also be made on rivers, lakes, and coastal regions in towns such as Copenhagen and Odense.

Copenhagen travel In Copenhagen you buy tickets singly or, much more cheaply, at a discount from bus drivers or at S-train (*S-tog*) stations. Tickets are valid on both buses and S-trains for an hour in the central traffic area. You yourself have to stamp the time on them by means of an automatic machine when boarding a bus or a train (on stations use the yellow, not the red, machine for central area travel). Failure to stamp the ticket involves a 50 kr fine. Supplementary fares are paid for travel outside the central zone. 'Tourist tickets' providing out-of-town excursions at extremely reasonable rates can be bought from hotel porters as well as at railway stations etc. Admission to places of interest is often included in the price.

For private-car touring and for camping and caravanning see Motoring, below.

Where to stay
Denmark's attractive accommodation range includes hotels of many sorts, country inns, motels, 'holiday centres', pensions, furnished

holiday apartments and chalets of various types, farmhouses, first-rate Youth Hostels, and in Copenhagen 'sleep-ins' and other accommodation for younger, less well-off travellers. A hotel guide that lists accommodation of virtually every sort can be obtained free from Danish tourist offices.

Hotels Denmark has no official hotel classifications. Prices however are competitive and give a good general idea of each establishment's standards and facilities. They fall into three main categories – de luxe, normal, and modest. Standards are mostly very high, and prices pretty reasonable. Hotels that are members of the Inter group sell cheaply a 'bonus check' entitling holders to 20% reductions.

Establishments described as 'mission' hotels are in reality a special type of family-run concern, not parts of some vast nationwide chain. All have a basically religious and 'temperance' background. But note that to the Danes, sensible about these as about so many other matters, 'temperance' means drinking nothing stronger than beer or wine, while the religious interest is limited to a bible (in Danish) within reach of your bed and a very discreet card giving you the time of morning prayers should you wish to attend. Being run by individual families, who have often been in control for generations, the 25 *missionshoteller* (as the Danes call them) are appreciably cheaper than comparable ordinary hotels. As a result they are usually heavily booked – in Copenhagen throughout the year, and elsewhere at Christmas, Easter, and during the Danish schools' summer holidays (mid-June to late August).

Pensions is the term given by Danes to establishments which in the UK are often called guesthouses. In Denmark they vary from places which are really small – sometimes not-so-small – family-run hotels to families who let one or two bedrooms. Many larger establishments of the first type are included in the hotel lists supplied free by Danish-Scandinavian tourist offices. For the smaller places you must enquire from local tourist information offices, either in advance or on the spot. Standards are usually very high, though the number of rooms with private bath is naturally very limited, and prices little if anything below what you pay in many hotels.

Country inns Many inns are extremely attractive old buildings, with facilities completely up-to-date and sometimes modern additions. As bases for touring and for activities such as fishing they can be ideal. Except in one or two that have become specially popular, prices are reasonable. Most inns are fairly small, and overnight stays need to be booked in advance. But midday and evening meals are always available. If you are driving through Denmark and want to eat well you can rarely do better than pulling up at a place marked *Kro*. Danish/Scandinavian tourist offices have free leaflets giving inns' locations and bookings can be made through various regional associations. Danish NTOs can let you have their addresses.

Motels cater mainly, but not entirely, for motorists. Some, located just outside big towns including Copenhagen, provide good accommodation at rates that may be lower than inside the city limits. All provide facilities specially designed for motorists, usually with a petrol and repair garage next door to them.

Farmhouses provide a form of accommodation that has proved enormously popular with visitors from many countries – not least those with young children. You book through regional associations, mainly in Jutland or on Funen, for stays of a week or a fortnight. Several UK firms, notably DFDS Danish Seaways, offer very reasonably-priced packages. Details are available from Danish (or Scandinavian) tourist offices.

Many farmhouses also offer self-catering accommodation in chalets or apartments either self-contained or involving some degree of sharing with the farm family. These can be booked through local associations, whose addresses can be obtained from Danish/Scandinavian tourist offices.

Summer cottages in Denmark means small bungalows, often built of wood and sometimes very small indeed, usually sited within reach of a good beach, and intended for family holidays. They are always efficiently equipped and comfortable. Some are decidedly luxurious. They can be rented in many resorts, and several British firms offer packages that include them. If thinking of making your own rental arrangements you are recommended to use one of the organisations whose names and addresses you can get from a Danish or Scandinavian tourist office.

Holiday centres is another term which in Denmark does not mean quite what you might think. It refers to mixtures of hotels and summer cottages. All living units have kitchenettes where you can do your own cooking. Alternatively, you can eat in the centre's restaurant or cafeteria. Prices range from extremely reasonable to moderate, with accommodation for anything from two to eight people.

Youth hostels Denmark has over 80 youth hostels at strategic locations throughout the country. Standards in general are exceptionally high. Dormitory accommodation for men and women is sometimes available, but most space in modern hostels is used for rooms containing four beds which can also be used by families with children under 15. Danish youth hostels place no restrictions on age, nor on how you travel. Everyone is welcome, and hostel tours by car, cycle, or bus, as well as on foot, are extremely popular among the Danes themselves. Membership of your national youth hostel association or an international youth hostel card is essential. You can buy one after arrival from the Danish YHA (Herbergs-Ringen) or from one of the larger hostels, such as that at Esbjerg. You can get detailed information from our own YHA or Denmark's.

Anyone not familiar with Europe's highly-developed youth hostel system should realise that the non-profitmaking hostels provide beds, possibly several to a room, washing and cooking facilities, and sometimes simple meals at the lowest possible prices. Guests do the cleaning themselves each morning, and wash up after meals.

In Denmark hostel accommodation is much cheaper than anything except camping.

'Sleep-ins' and other youth accommodation are available in Copenhagen. The city's special Youth Information Centre 'Huset' (or 'Use It': the word really means 'the house') will tell you what is available.

Advance booking of accommodation There is no central booking agency. The more expensive hotels are represented in the USA and Canada as well as Britain, and travel agents will know how to make bookings quickly. For the less expensive you mostly have to make bookings yourself. In most of Denmark local tourist information offices help you. In Copenhagen, however, the tourist office does not make reservations of any sort. Rooms in hotels or private houses can be obtained there by personal application to the SAS Hotel Booking Office at the airport or at Kiosk P on the Central Station. For youth hostel bookings you should write to individual hostels. Enclose international reply-paid coupons to cover postage.

Campsites See Motoring, camping, and caravanning.

Where to eat
Restaurants exist in large numbers in all towns and tourist areas, main stations, and ferries. Snackbars, called *cafeterias*, are also plentiful, and in towns you can usually buy take-away *smørrebrød* (Danish open sandwiches: try not to annoy normally very placid Danes by using the Swedish term *smörgåsbord* for them).

When looking for somewhere to eat remember that if Danes go to a restaurant they are often planning to eat a festive meal. Helpings are apt to be enormous, and prices fairly high. Finding less expensive meals depends largely on knowing the Danes' eating habits, described in Life Danish Style, below. Places serving a

Danish 'cold table' (*kolde bord*) at not too high a price often provide the best solutions, and give you not only a tremendous choice of what you eat but also a good view of typical Danish food. A 'cold table' is not entirely cold. It normally includes a choice of hot dishes, a huge choice of *smørrebrød*, and cheese, fruit, and possibly other desserts as well. The cold table at Copenhagen's Central Station is deservedly famous. Other big stations also have good restaurants.

If you want a restaurant meal but do not want to pay too much, ask for the 'daily card' (*dagens kort*), not the 'menu'. The daily card gives details of the table d'hôte (blue plate) meal, with a limited number of choices at a fixed price. 'Menu' to a Dane means the often much more expensive à la carte list.

Cafeterias provide inexpensive meals. The hot *pølser* (frankfurters) sold from street stalls in lots of places make the cheapest snacks of all. You can eat them plain, or inside a roll like a hot dog.

When you are thirsty

Cafés and bars where you can order drinks and sit and talk or just sit and watch the world go by are plentiful in towns and holiday areas. Coffee, chocolate, and tea (served English-fashion if you ask for it with milk) are available, as well as alcoholic drinks. Prices are mostly above British and North American standards: imported drinks like whisky are very expensive.

For your evening's entertainment

Apart from theatre, opera, ballet, cinema, and concerts all major towns and holiday areas are well provided with evening and night entertainment which ranges from dinner-dance and floorshow establishments where formal clothes are essential to discos, jazz clubs, and other places where music is the chief attraction, as well as to noisy, lively spots, which may be thoroughly well-behaved or cheerfully disreputable. In many provincial towns as well as Copenhagen you can drink or drink and dance the night through until the first bars open next morning. Because of high drink prices, however, evenings of this sort are apt to strike visitors as pretty costly. You can gamble on a limited scale at the Marienlyst Hotel's casino at Elsinore. Tourist information offices provide sound information and advice about all types of nightspot.

Information after arrival

We have referred to the local tourist information offices many times. Perhaps this is the point at which to make it clear that they really do solve almost every problem and answer every query that a visitor may have. They make travelling in Denmark exceptionally easy and pleasant. English is spoken in all of them as a matter of course.

You and your money

The Danish unit of currency is the *krone* ('crown': plural *kroner*), abbreviated kr, divided into 100 *øre* (singular also *øre*). 'Dkr', 'Skr', and 'Nkr' distinguishes Danish, Swedish, and Norwegian crowns. Coins are: 5, 10, and 25 *øre*; and 1, 5, and 10 kroner. Banknotes come in denominations of 20, 50, 100, 500, and 1000 kr. For an indication of current exchange rates see Prices.

You can import unlimited Danish and foreign currency into Denmark, but must not export more than 5000 kr in Danish banknotes unless you have imported at least that much.

Both banknotes and traveller's cheques can be exchanged at frontier exchange offices, including Copenhagen's Central Station, Kastrup Airport, and many international ferries; at exchange offices in large towns and tourist centres; and also in some of the larger hotels and, of course, banks. All give almost exactly the same rates.

Organising your sightseeing

No problem. Consult the local tourist information office. If possible, however, have a bit of a look-round on foot first. It is silly to spend all your time on a coach tour in, say, Copenhagen – and then regret that you did not take one of the delightful boat trips.

Practical details

Children are outstandingly well looked after in Denmark and travelling with them is no problem. Hotels supply cots and restaurants high chairs as a matter of course. Hotels, ferries, etc often have special playrooms. Hotels often give large reductions for children. Babysitters who speak good English are readily available – consult the local tourist office, or your hotel. In main stations and on major ferries you will find 'mothers' rooms' with facilities for changing nappies, warming feeds, etc. Babyfoods common in UK and North America are on sale everywhere, and wherever you go you will find a vast range of facilities designed specially for children. Up to four they travel free on trains, etc, and half-price from four to 12.

Correspondence Letters can be sent 'poste restante' to any post office (but address them 'Central Post Office' in large towns). Take your passport when collecting mail. Thomas Cook and American Express will also hold mail for you if you are travelling with them (or hold an American Express card). US and Canadian Embassies can also be used by US and Canadian nationals, but have no forwarding arrangements. Allow at least 7-10 days for letters from the UK or North America.

Disabled travellers receive plenty of help in Denmark. Railways and airports make special arrangements if notified in advance. Lists of the 150-odd hotels with special facilities for the disabled are available: also of disabled people's holiday centres, places where wheelchairs can be hired, etc. The organisations most active in this sphere are the National Association of the Disabled (*Landsforeningen af Vanføre*) and the Society and Home for the Disabled (*Samfundet og Hjemmet for Vanføre*). A centre run by *Dansk Folke-Ferie* at Karlslunde near Copenhagen is open to foreign disabled visitors all the year and they can use other of the society's centres outside 21 June-12 August. Some campsites run by FDM, the Danish motoring organisation, are equipped to deal with disabled visitors. Consult any Danish/Scandinavian tourist office for up-to-date information. In London the Royal Association for Disability and Rehabilitation also provides information and advice about holidays.

Dry cleaning can be arranged through the larger town and resort hotels, or directly through dry cleaning shops.

Electricity 220 volts and 50 cycles everywhere, with 110 volt sockets available for shavers in some hotels and campsites. Danish plugs, however, are different from British and North American.

Emergencies Dial 000 (there is no charge) for police, fire, or ambulance. For less immediate emergencies ask advice from the tour firm's rep if you are on a package tour, or from your hotel concierge, campsite warden, farmhouse host, etc – or from the local tourist office. In the event of serious upsets (if you lose your passport or are arrested, for instance) contact your country's nearest consular representative. Consular and diplomatic representatives cannot supply money or make bookings for you, whatever your needs. But they can supply temporary travel documents, inform your family, help you cable for additional funds, give you names and addresses of lawyers, etc.

Language English is spoken by almost everyone – or so you feel after a few days in Denmark.

Laundry The large hotels do it well. But it is easier to take a little detergent and do your own. Chambermaids will help cope with ironing.

Lavatories (men's and ladies' rooms) You will see public lavatories, marked *WC* (pronounced *vee-see*) or *Toiletter,* in some places. Elsewhere go into any bar or restaurant or hotel. A small charge is made for washing facilities.

Meet the Danes Local tourist offices in a few places (not Copenhagen) can arrange for visitors to meet a Danish family over a cup of coffee. You must visit the tourist office in person at least 24 hours in advance.

Museums and art galleries Opening-times vary, with many establishments opening from 10.00 to about 16.00 or 17.00 and others remaining closed until 13.00 and opening for the afternoon only. Some close one day a week, usually Monday. Some also stay open in the evenings. Get information locally.

Photography There are no special restrictions. Popular types of amateur film can be bought almost everywhere.

Places of worship St Alban's *very* English-looking Anglican church on Langelinie is one of Copenhagen's landmarks. In July there are international services in Arhus. There are synagogues in Copenhagen and other main towns. Consult local tourist offices.

Post offices Open Monday-Friday 09.00 or 10.00-17.00 or 18.00: Saturdays 09.00-12.00 or closed. In Copenhagen the Central Station Post Office opens 08.00-23.00 Monday-Saturday and 08.00-21.00 on Sundays and public holidays. You can usually buy stamps at hotel and campsite reception desks, kiosks which sell postcards and souvenirs, etc, as well as at post offices.

Public holidays 1981 1 January, 16 April (Maundy Thursday), 17, 19, and 20 April (Easter), 15 May (Great Prayer Day), 28 May (Ascension Day), 5 June (from 12.00 on: Constitution Day), 7 and 8 June (Whitsun), 25 and 26 December.

Shopping and banking hours Shopping hours vary, but 09.00-17.30 on Monday-Thursday, 09.00-19.00 or 20.00 on Friday, and 09.00-12.00 or 14.00 on Saturday constitute fairly normal hours. Some supermarkets, souvenir kiosks, etc may stay open late and on Sundays. Banks are normally open 09.30-16.00 (09.30-18.00 on Thursday) except for Saturday and Sunday, when they are closed.

Telephones are fully automatic, with two-digit area codes and six-digit numbers. Call boxes take $2 \times 25 \not{c}$re, 1 kr, or 5 kr coins, which are *not* returned if you get no answer (so start with the smallest possible coins). For UK you dial 00944 and for North America 0091.

Tipping In general – don't. Leave 1-2 kr if you have used the washroom in the Ladies' or Gents'. Do not tip hairdressers or theatre and cinema ushers. Railway porters (you book them in advance) have fixed charges. The only people who expect tips are country taxi-drivers without meters – 15%.

Youth and student travel Special facilities and reduced rates are available. Danish and Scandinavian tourist offices in UK and North America and Copenhagen's Youth Information Centre can supply details. The Centre does everything a young traveller can need. It finds cheap accommodation, advises on where to eat (including specialities such as oriental or kosher food), gives you information about sightseeing and excursions, provides lockers for luggage, runs a 'poste restante' service, arranges meetings and the exchange of firsthand travel experience, and operates a 'rides offered' service for would-be hitch-hikers.

Radio news in English is broadcast at 08.15 every weekday morning. Brief weekend traffic reports are included on Fridays in summer.

Prices

The following must be treated as being for guidance only. In modern conditions all prices are liable to sudden change, not least because of abrupt alterations in exchange rates. The prices we quote were as correct as we could make them in spring 1980.

Exchange rates £1=13 kr, 1 kr=8p; US$1=6.02 kr, 1 kr=16¢; CA$1=5.10 kr, 1 kr=20¢.

General price levels Most things cost the same as you would expect to pay in the UK or North America or maybe a little more.

Air travel London-Copenhagen return: 1st-class £382, full-rate economy-class £218, one-month economy £170, APEX £97, minimum-rated packages from about £85.

New York-Copenhagen round trip: 1st-class US$1788, full-rate economy-class $784-992 or $694-878 according to airline, 14-45 day 'excursion' $724-852 or $640-754, APEX $634, Mini-Fare $370-438 according to season, public charters from $429.

Toronto-Copenhagen round trip: 1st-class CA$2172, full-rate economy $1030, 7-60 day APEX $639, youth $639-849.

Copenhagen-Rønne (Bornholm): full-rate return 484 kr.

Rail travel London-Copenhagen via Harwich-Esbjerg: one-way £40 (minimum-grade on-board accommodation), via Hook of Holland £53, via Ostend £58. Copenhagen-Esbjerg: 2nd-class single 140 kr.

Bus and coach London-Copenhagen: one-way £24 (Magic Bus). Inside Denmark, as for rail travel.

Ferries Harwich-Esbjerg one way: passengers £27-£63 according to cabin and season, cars £46-nil according to season, height of car, and number of accompanying passengers, without distinction of length. Great Belt (Store Bælt) Passengers 17 kr, cars 79 kr.

Other transport in Denmark Taxis 8 kr+4 kr per km. Car hire from about 1250 kr per week, unlimited mileage. Cycle hire 10-50 kr per day, 50-250 per week. Canoe hire per week for two people, including safety gear, tent, camp fees, return freight 1100 kr; 60 kr for each additional child under 12.

Accommodation Hotels in Copenhagen, double room with bath: top grade 450-700 kr, medium 350-450 kr, modest 160-350 kr.

Hotels outside Copenhagen: top grade 270-400 kr, medium 155-300 kr, modest 137-170 kr. Prices all include all taxes: breakfasts are also included in Copenhagen, but not necessarily elsewhere.

Inns, double room with bath: allow 200-400 kr in top grade, 150-250 kr in others, though there are wide variations. Many provide room and all meals for 200 kr per day per person.

Summer cottages 400-2200 kr per week (4 beds). Farmhouse holidays 735-840 kr per week full board, 630-735 kr half board. Farms' self-catering 550-920 kr per week (4 beds). Holiday centres 750-2000 kr per week (up to 6 beds). Youth hostels 18-23 kr overnight, breakfast 14 kr, dinner 20 kr.

Meals and drinks Main meal: cheap 20-30 kr, medium 30-100 kr. Two hot *pølser* from street stall 8 kr. Coffee (pot) 10-15 kr, beer (glass) 8.50 kr, coke 5 kr. Bottle of whisky in shop 110-150 kr.

Motoring and camping Petrol 4.60 kr per litre. Campsites 14-16 kr per day per person.

Essential addresses

If you need the addresses of tour operators, ferry companies, or airlines flying from your own country you can get them from your travel agent – who may, in any case, be able to answer your queries or clear up any difficulties you may have.

In Britain

Danish National Tourist Office, 169/173 Regent Street, London W1R 8PY

Royal Danish Embassy and Consulate-General, 55 Sloane Street, London SW1

Danish Institute, 3 Doune Terrace, Edinburgh 3

SAS Scandinavian Airlines, 52-3 Conduit Street, London W1R 0AY

AA, PO Box 50, Basingstoke, Hants, RG21 2ED

Camping Club of Great Britain, 11 Lower Grosvenor Place, London SW1W 0EY

Caravan Club, East Grinstead House, East Grinstead, W. Sussex, RH19 1UA

Europ Assistance, 269-273 High Street, Croydon, Surrey, CR0 1QH

RAC, RAC House, Lansdowne Road, Croydon, Surrey, CR9 1JA

Youth Hostels Association (England and Wales), 14 Southampton Street, London WC2

Scottish Youth Hostels Association, 7 Glebe Crescent, Stirling

BR Continental, PO Box 2, Victoria Station, London SW1V 6YL

Europabus, c/o National Travel, Victoria Coach Station, Buckingham Palace Road, London SW1W 9TP

Magic Bus, 66 Shaftesbury Avenue, London W1

Scantours Ltd, 8 Spring Garden, London SW1

Edward Stanford Ltd, 12 Long Acre, London WC2 9LP

Norwegian State Railways, 21 Cockspur Street, London SW1

Customs & Excise, King's Beam House, Mark Lane, London EC3 7HE

In the USA

Danish National Tourist Office, 75 Rockefeller Plaza, NYC 10019

Royal Danish Consulate-General, 3400 Wilshire Boulevard, Suite 904, Los Angeles, CA 90010

SAS Scandinavian Airlines, SAS Building, 138-02 Queens Boulevard, Jamaica, NY 11435

Britrail, 270 Madison Avenue, NYC 10016

CIEE, 777 United Nations Plaza, NYC 10017

Consumers' Union, Mt Vernon, NY 10550

IAMAT, 350 Fifth Avenue (Suite 5620), NYC 10001

World Medical Association, 1841 Broadway, NYC 10023

American Youth Hostels Association, 132 Spring Street, NYC 10012

US Customs, Department of the Treasury, Washington DC 20229

In Canada

Danish National Tourist Office, 151 Bloor Street West, Toronto, Ont M5S 1S4

Royal Danish Embassy and Consulate-General, 85 Range Road, Ottawa, K1N 8J5

SAS Scandinavian Airlines, 800 Dorchester Street West, Montreal, Quebec

Britrail, 55 Eglinton Avenue East, Toronto 12, Ont M4P 1G8

IAMAT, 1268 St Clair Avenue West, Toronto, Ont M6E 1B9

Voyageur Travel Insurance, 75 Selby Road, Brampton, Ont L6V 9Z9

Canadian Youth Hostels Association, 333 River Road, Vanier City, Ottawa

Canada Customs have offices in Halifax, Quebec, Montreal, Ottawa, Toronto, Hamilton, London, Windsor, Winnipeg, Regina, Calgary, Vancouver.

In Denmark

British Embassy and Consulate-General, 36-40 Kastelsvej, DK-2100 Copenhagen Ø

Canadian Embassy, Prinsesse Maries Alle 2, DK-1908 Copenhagen V

US Embassy, Dag Hammarskjölds Alle 24, DK-2100 Copenhagen Ø

British Airways, Vesterbrogade 2, DK-1620 Copenhagen V

Air Canada, Vester Farimagsgade 1-3, DK-7606 Copenhagen V

Northwest Orient Airlines, Vester Farimagsgade 7, DK-1606 Copenhagen V

Tourist Information Office, Banegårdspladsen 2, DK-1570, Copenhagen V (by the Central Station)

Herbergs-Ringen, Vesterbrogade 35, DK-1620 Copenhagen V

Students' Club, Købmagergade 26C, DK-1150 Copenhagen K

Youth Information Centre 'Huset', Magstræde 14, DK-1204 Copenhagen V

Landsforeningen af Vanføre (National Association of the Disabled), Hans Knudsens Plads 1, DK-2100 Copenhagen Ø

Samfundet og Hjemmet for Vanføre (Society and Home for the Disabled), Borgervænget 7, DK-2100 Copenhagen V

FDM (Forenede Danske Motorejere), Blegdamsvej 124, DK-2100, Copenhagen Ø

Dansk Folke-Ferie, Kampmannsgade 3, DK-1604 Copenhagen V

Motoring, camping and caravanning

Motoring in Denmark has many pleasant aspects. The rolling countryside, with its trim, colourful farms, woods, and heathland, is much more attractively varied than foreigners usually imagine. Apart from four or five large towns and a few main through-routes traffic is rarely heavy. Even when it is, there are scores of quiet byways where cars are scarce. Wayside inns (*kro*) make pleasant stopping-places for meals or coffee. And there are lots of places worth visiting.

Taking your car to Denmark

Ferries from UK (listed above under Getting to Denmark) all carry cars. In addition you can, if you wish, use one of the car-ferry routes to Norway, Sweden, or West Germany as part of a tour taking in Denmark. If you are coming from some other part of Europe there are numerous car-carrying ferry routes from Norway, Sweden, West Germany, East Germany, and Poland. A car or camper or trailer-caravan tour taking in other countries as well as Denmark is very easy indeed.

Documents and insurance

If you take your own car from UK or elsewhere you will need your registration certificate ('log book'), state or national full (not provisional) driving licence, and ordinary insurance certificate. If the vehicle is not your own you must have a letter of authority from the owner and the log book (or a photocopy). UK insurance now covers basic legal requirements for third-party cover in all Common Market countries such as Denmark – but not accidental damage to your own vehicle, fire, theft, or personal accident, let alone the cost of repairs done abroad, flying out spares, bringing home a damaged car, etc.

You may therefore think it worth extending your UK cover by means of a 'green card' and buying special insurance to cover possibly heavy costs of repairs etc done abroad. Your insurers will normally provide a green card for a small fee, but apply in good time. The motoring organisations, Caravan Club, Camping Club, and other bodies arrange insurance of the second type. Europ Assistance do it cheaply and very well. See Insurance, above.

Driving in Denmark

Roads and signposting Even the most minor roads are usually very well built and surfaced. Fast motorways link major towns: no tolls are charged on them. Where bridges are still lacking, fast, efficient ferries make it possible to reach even the smallest islands easily and quickly and to tour well away from the busiest regions.

Destination signs mostly follow international patterns and are clear and efficient on the open road. In towns, however, they are sometimes placed so low that cars and people hide them completely, and are sometimes so positioned that you drive through a crossroads before discovering that you ought to have turned off.

Roads are numbered and the numbers shown clearly on both signposts and maps. Main road numbers carry A-prefixes and may also have separate E-numbers when they form part of European through-routes. On minor roads simple finger-posts are usually adequate to prevent you losing your way.

Some road signs tend to use words. They include:

Spaerret	Road closed
Halve Vejbane Spaerret	(Half road closed) Single-lane traffic
Ensrettet	One-way traffic
Cykelsti	Cycle track (cycles and mopeds only)
Cykelsti Ender	Cycle track ends (most important: here cyclists pour onto the road)

Rabatten Blφd or	Soft verge
Rabatten er Blφd	
Vejarbejde	Road works in progress
Omkφrsel	Diversion
Kun Personvogne	Private cars only

One special emblem-sign that you may see occasionally in woodland is a simple solid red disc. It means 'no road for cars'. Cyclists can still use the track.

Ferry bookings inside Denmark In summer, advance bookings for vehicles are absolutely essential for Great Belt crossings and advisable on most other routes. Reservations on ferries operated by Danish Railways can be made at any station. A booklet provided free by tourist offices tells you where to phone for the others.

Attractive touring regions The regions with the most attractive scenery are the Rebild Hills, the Silkeborg Hills and lakes, the fjords and hills spread almost all along Jutland's east coast, the South Funen Hills, northern Zealand, and the island of Bornholm.

Maps
If you intend going only to Copenhagen and a few other large cities or main resorts almost any road map of Denmark will serve. But, if you want to get to know the countryside well, the ten 1:150,000 maps (about $2\frac{1}{4}$ miles to 1 inch) published by the Geodætisk Institut are ideal. They are among the world's best touring maps, and contain a wealth of information. They can be bought easily in Danish bookshops, from UK motoring organisations, and from the London map and guidebook specialists Edward Stanford Ltd.

Breakdown and accident
Free breakdown assistance is available for members of the AA, RAC, AAA, or CAA. Roadside help and towage is provided mainly by the remarkable Falck organisation, a private company which also runs the country's ambulance and fire brigades and provides much of its insurance. Passers-by will phone on your behalf. The Danish motoring organisation FDM also helps visiting motorists.

Accident procedure is fundamentally the same as in other countries, except that it is normal to allow the other driver to copy your name and address and your insurance company's name and address from formal documents (such as your driving licence and insurance certificate) rather than to write them down for him.

Call the police (as well as an ambulance) if anyone is injured, and always try to obtain witnesses.

Laws
In Denmark you drive on the right and overtake on the left. Be specially careful when turning right in towns. Cyclists going straight on on your inside have right of way.

Speed limits are 100 kph (62 mph) on motorways, 80 kph (50 mph) on ordinary roads, and 60 kph (35 mph) in built-up areas. Cars towing caravans or other trailers are limited to 70 kph (33 mph) and must leave room for overtaking cars to pull in in front of them. On-the-spot speeding fines can be very heavy. If you cannot pay, the car may be impounded.

Overtaking is forbidden if it involves crossing even a single solid white line, and also at approaches to pedestrian crossings. Indicators are not necessarily used if intentions are clear.

Priority rules are different from Britain's and similar to Canada's and the USA's. Give way to all traffic coming from your right. In roundabouts vehicles in the roundabout have priority. In open country, minor roads joining priority routes are marked with 'Stop' signs. Cars must always give way to buses pulling out from roadside stops.

Headlights You must always drive after dusk, or in mist, fog, heavy rain, snow, etc with dipped headlights, not sidelights. Left-dipping headlights are illegal. On British cars you must either tape over part of your headlight glass or fit lenses which change the dipped beam's direction. These can be bought from garages, accessory shops, the motoring organisations, etc.

Motorcyclists must at all times use dipped headlights and wear crash helmets.

Seat belts must be worn in front seats.

Parking is stricly controlled, especially in Copenhagen. Wrongly-parked cars may be towed away and only released after payment of towage, garaging, and a heavy fine. PARKERING FORBUDT means No Parking. STANDSNING FORBUDT indicates No Stopping. In both cases however you are allowed up to 3 minutes for (un)loading and picking up or setting down passengers. Cars can be parked with two wheels on the pavement only in areas where police regulations permit and no inconvenience is caused to pedestrians. Meters operate in some streets between 09.00 and 18.00 (Saturdays 09.00-13.00: Sundays no restrictions). They take 25-øre and 1-krone coins. Maximum stay is 3 hours.

Signs indicating limited waiting use black lettering for Monday-Friday, black with brackets for Saturday, and red for Sunday. 'K1.5' in Danish means 'five o'clock. '2 timer' means 'two hours'. Parking discs are needed in limited-waiting areas. You set the disc to show the time you left the car. Discs can be obtained from police stations, post offices, petrol stations, and some banks. In some streets DATOPARKERING or DATOSTOP indicates that you park outside even-numbered houses on even dates and vice versa.

Drinking and driving Penalties for driving under the influence of drink are extremely severe, and the alcohol limit low enough for one drink to be the limit. If your friends are drinking and you do not wish to, turn your empty glass upside down. It is a universally understood and respected sign. An almost alcohol-free and pleasant-tasting beer-substitute called *lys øl* ('light ale') is available as an alternative.

Warning triangles The use of red warning triangles is obligatory when cars have to stop on the road. The triangle must be placed 50 m behind the stopped vehicle (100 m on motorways).

Using your horn is completely forbidden except in case of danger. Whenever possible, flash your headlights instead.

Campsites
Denmark has some of the best and best-organised campsites in Europe. Some 500 of them have been inspected and approved by the Danish National Camping Committee, and are efficiently signposted from nearby main roads. They are divided into 1-, 2-, and 3-star categories. The 1-star camps possess the essential minimum of sanitary installations, drinking water, and so on. 2-star sites have, in addition, windbreaks, showers, laundry facilities and a provision store within 2 km. Places awarded 3-stars have everything: about a hundred are so well equipped that they stay open all year. A number of sites run by FDM, the Danish motoring association, are reserved for members of motoring organisations affiliated to the AIT, such as the AA, RAC, AAA, CAA, etc.

An international camping carnet, obtainable by members from motoring organisations, national camping clubs, etc, is obligatory – though visitors can also buy an emergency camping pass, covering themselves and their immediate family for a month, at the first approved site they stay at.

For Motels, see Where to stay, above.

Life Danish Style
History

Archaeological finds show that about 4000 years ago a race of farming folk moved northward into Jutland and the Danish islands. During the Bronze Age, 1500—500 BC Denmark was at the crossroads of north-south and east-west trade and obviously prosperous. Prosperity returned during the Viking period when trade as well as war and plunder took the sailor-warrior-merchants to many distant lands. At the peak of Viking expansion the Danish King Canute the Great (1018-35: the Canute we remember in Britain) ruled an empire which extended from the southern provinces of Sweden to the west of England. England was lost soon after Canute's death but expansion occurred again in the 13th and 14th centuries. King Valdemar Sejr (1202-1241) ruled south Sweden, the whole south Baltic seaboard including Holstein and parts of Mecklenburg and Pomerania, and Estonia (not yet converted to Christianity) as well as Denmark. Though Estonia was lost, his daughter married Haakon VI of Norway, eventually succeeding to both thrones.

The Faroes, Iceland, and Greenland became Danish along with Norway. In 1389 Margrethe invaded and conquered Sweden too.

Sweden, never very strongly held by the Danes, was lost in 1658. Norway however was not detached from Denmark until after the Napoleonic wars (in which Denmark suffered severely at British hands—it was at the battle of Copenhagen that Nelson put his telescope to his blind eye to avoid seeing his commander-in-chief's signal to break off the engagement). Norway became part of Sweden in 1814. Iceland asserted her independence in 1946, but Greenland and the Faroes are still ruled from Denmark.

Serfdom was abolished in 1788, an event commemorated by an obelisk still standing in Copenhagen's Vesterbrogade opposite the Central Station. When the system of communal tillage ended most peasant farmers moved their homes to their outlying fields and gave the Danish landscape, dotted with isolated farms, its present typical appearance. Many later emigrated to the USA and Canada.

During the Napoleonic wars the British blockade, the destruction of the Danish fleet at the battle of Copenhagen, and the severe bombardment of Copenhagen in 1807 did serious damage. In 1813 Denmark was literally bankrupt. But that did not prevent the Danes from introducing universal elementary education in the following year.

It was another disaster—the loss of the South Jutland province of Schleswig-Holstein to the Prussians in 1864 after a short but expensive war, that proved the making of modern Denmark. In the

1860s the Folk High School movement, started in 1844, began to spread throughout the country providing a remarkable system of adult education that still flourishes today. In 1866 Denmark's first cooperative store opened at Thisted in Jutland—and began a movement which is still one of the corner-stones of efficient Danish farming. The Danish Heath Society was founded in the same year to ensure previously unknown productivity for the soil, and in that period, too, the country's sports clubs, which still do so much to ensure a healthy nation, began to be formed.

This was the beginning of Denmark's modern prosperity. Extensive industrialisation began soon afterwards, quickly gathered momentum, and is now advancing very rapidly indeed. The overwhelming bulk of the population lives and works in towns. Yet despite the continuous loss of farm workers and the deliberate discouragement of farm productivity because of marketing difficulties, farm production is still rising steadily.

During World War II the Danes found themselves forced to surrender to the invading Nazis. But the overwhelming bulk of the population remained strongly pro-Ally and quietly and determinedly, in true Danish manner, did all they could to obstruct the Nazis. In the postwar years the country's standard of living has risen higher than ever, though inflation has been a major problem. Denmark joined the Common Market at the same time as Britain.

The Arts

Architecture has flourished in Denmark for many centuries. Though the names of few practitioners will be known to ordinary Britons—with the possible exception of the modern architect-designer Arne Jacobsen—there is a huge amount worth seeing. It dates from Viking days right down to the present.

The story begins with the camp at Trelleborg on Zealand and other Viking remains. It continues with the many fine castles and manor houses scattered all over Denmark but particularly frequent in southern Funen, where moated Egeskov is the finest example of all. Denmark's extraordinary architect-king, Christian IV (1588-1648), left a considerable number of fine buildings to posterity, including Copenhagen's Stock Exchange.

In Aalborg, Aarhus, Roskilde, Ribe, and elsewhere you will find delightful cathedrals dating back to the Middle Ages. Attractive, colourful village churches can be found throughout the country: they include the one at Jelling beside which Denmark's first king is buried and seven defensive circular churches, four of them on the remote island of Bornholm. Timbered farmhouses and village dwellings, black and white or gaily coloured, are even more numerous. And to complete the story there is a remarkable assortment of modern buildings that are not only imaginative and unusual but also thoroughly attractive, enjoyable, and practical. A few are mentioned in the text. But if you want to make a serious study of modern Danish architecture you should ask the National Tourist Board for advice on where to go and what to see. The Danes have long specialised in organising 'study tours'.

The fine arts have similarly flourished in Denmark during recent centuries, though only the sculptor Bertel Thorvaldsen (1770-1844) has ever become world famous. Even without visiting the big art galleries you will see a huge amount of sculpture used to decorate buildings and public places—and much of it is decidedly good. In painting the best-known names include: Michael and Anna Ancher, C. W. Eckersberg, Julius Exner, P. S. Krøyer, Johannes Larsen, Vilhelm Landstrøm, Olaf Rude, and J. F. Willumsen. Among sculptors Jean Gauguin (son of the French Impressionist), Kai Nielsen, Vilhelm Bissen, Astrid Noack, and E. Utzon-Frank are well known.

In applied art Denmark occupies a very high position. Years ago Danish cabinet-makers teamed up with architects (all of whom are trained also as designers) to make Danish handmade furniture as good as any available anywhere in the world. As long ago as the 1930s Kay Bojesen started his experiments with cutlery design that resulted in the mass of stainless steel tableware now produced by hundreds of manufacturers. The famous silversmith Georg Jensen gave silverware new dimensions. The ceramic products of world-famous firms such as the Royal Copenhagen Porcelain Factory and Bing & Grøndal and of individual designers have put Denmark in a class apart.

In literature Hans Andersen is perhaps the only widely known name, though the scientist Piet Hein's English 'Grooks' (as he calls his amusing poems) are appreciated in many countries. But despite the smallness of their market—even today only about 6 million people read Danish—there have always been plenty of writers and poets. The best known, apart from Hans Andersen, are: Ludwig Holberg, Johannes V. Jensen (a Nobel Prize winner), Martin Andersen Nexø, Kai Munk (murdered by the Nazis), Karen Blixen (who wrote in English), Nis Petersen, Hans Kirk, Jacob Paludan, Soya, and Martin A. Hansen. All are available in English translation.

Music thrives in Denmark, with orchestras and numerous concerts not only in the main towns but in smaller places as well. Among Danish composers only Carl Nielsen is well known to British audiences. But the Royal Danish Ballet holds a unique position in its own world. Not only are its standards extremely high, it also possesses a repertory going back almost 200 years, enabling us to trace in one company the changes made since the great Taglioni revolutionised dancing in the early 19th century.

One other aspect of Denmark's music deserves mention—the little parish churches that you see dotted across the landscapes contain an inordinately large number of first-rate baroque organs. Special tours are occasionally organised for keen organists, both professional and amateur.

Sports

Swimming There are hundreds of beaches on Denmark's 7300km of coastline. Most are sandy, wide, and backed by dunes. The bathing season lasts from May to September.

On many beaches, especially along the wild West Jutland coast, car driving is permitted. There are speed limit signs on Fanø beach.

Nude bathing is officially permitted at a number of public beaches, on which you can take your clothes off or keep them on as you wish. Unofficially, people go naked elsewhere too but never, as the Danes express it, 'in a provocative manner'. In addition there are private nudist beaches and camps open only to holders of International Naturist Federation passes. Details change but the best up-to-date information is available through Danish Tourist Board offices, who provide an excellent free leaflet called 'Seaside Holiday'. Theoretically you can be fined for bathing naked at places where this is not officially permitted: in practice you will not be bothered if you make certain that other people on the beach accept the idea of your being nude. It should perhaps be added that nude bathing is a very old Scandinavian tradition: the only difference is that in times past the sexes were segregated.

Certain simple safety precautions are advised when bathing from Danish beaches. On Jutland's west coast the North Sea breakers can be enormous and currents in some places dangerous. Get knowledgeable local advice before deciding where to bathe. Remember that if a rescue operation becomes necessary you have to pay for it—and it can be very expensive.

Water-skiing is possible at virtually all popular resorts except those on the west Jutland coast. Specially good spots include Svendborg, several places on Bornholm, Aarhus Bay and Ebeltoft, the Limfjord, and the Silkeborg Lakes.

Scuba diving and underwater fishing are little practised in these northern waters.

Sailing is extremely popular. If you are not taking your own craft, lists of motor and sailboats hirers can be obtained from your DTB office or from local Tourist Association offices in Denmark. (See DTB leaflet 'Sailing in Denmark'.)

With 600 harbours Denmark provides plenty of variety. The only snags are: (1) that in enclosed waters you have to keep a careful lookout for the numerous ferries not always able to give sailing vessels right of way, and (2) if you tow a trailer-vessel of your own to Denmark, enquire first about slipway facilities as they are still somewhat scarce. Visitors' boats are regarded as sports equipment and imported duty free.

Fishing is one of Denmark's highlights. Sea fishing can be practised both from boats and from the shore, with catches including flatfish, cod, sea trout, mackerel, and gar-pike. In freshwater lakes and rivers rainbow trout, brown trout, and sea trout can be taken and the coarse fishing is as good as anywhere in Europe. Non-Scandinavians require a simple permit to fish in the sea. This can be obtained with the help of local tourist offices or applied for in advance from the Fiskeriinspektøren, Borgergade 16, DK-1300 Copenhagen K. State your nationality and passport number, and enclose an international reply coupon. Freshwater fishing involves obtaining prior permission from the landowner or angling club who own the fishing rights. You may simply have to pay a fee, or you may be obliged to take out temporary club membership. Again, the local tourist office will help you.

Golf Over 30 courses are scattered round Denmark. In every main town and tourist resort you are bound to be within easy reach of at least one. Standards are high, though the colder Danish winters usually make it impossible for courses to be in good condition except during late spring, early summer, and autumn. Visitors are welcome at most clubs and green fees are reasonable. Take your own clubs.

Tennis Every town and resort of any size will almost certainly have either outdoor or indoor tennis courts—if not both—belonging to clubs which always welcome foreign visitors. A small fee is sometimes charged for temporary membership.

Riding Horseback holidays have become very popular in Denmark in recent years. Touring, trekking, and training courses are all available. One of the most popular tours follows the old Military Road built through the middle of Jutland over a century ago. It is organised by the Jutland Riding Institute, Post Box 55, DK-7100 Vejle. But there are plenty of riding centres elsewhere: the National Tourist Office can give you up-to-date addresses.

Canoes and kayaks Kayaking is popular in Denmark, whose many lakes are ideal for the sport. Canoe touring on the rivers Guden, Sus, Skjern, and Stor (Gudenaaen, Susaaen, etc in Danish) are a Jutland speciality. In each case you can make a trip of about 160km.

At night you either camp on the bank or stay in one of the many local inns. Information can be obtained from the tourist office at Silkeborg, Jutland's main canoe-touring centre, and elsewhere.

Walking and cycling Country lanes and footpaths crossing hills and heaths and woodland make walking extremely pleasant in many parts of Denmark. Cycling is equally attractive, since it is quite possible to spend a whole day awheel and see no more than half a dozen cars at most. Bikes can be hired in most towns and resorts (for prices see p 25). Vejle, Viborg, and Aarhus tourist office provide excellent—and cheap—cycling tours specially suitable for families.

Spectator sports Apart from football, which is as popular in Denmark as everywhere else, the main spectator sport is trotting. There is a particularly popular course at Charlottenlund, just north of Copenhagen.

Nightlife and other entertainment

Nightspots of every sort flourish in Denmark. The choice is not quite so varied in main provincial towns and tourist resorts as in Copenhagen, but in these places there is always a fair selection. Hotel receptionists and tourist offices will bring you up to date with the latest 'in' spots.

Copenhagen and the other major towns have theatres which stage plays and opera. Concerts and Copenhagen's Royal Danish Ballet have already been mentioned. Cinemas are numerous in all main towns—over 50 in Copenhagen—and show many British and American films with the original soundtracks plus subtitles. Smoking is forbidden in all Danish cinemas, and it is usual to book tickets in advance. This can be done by telephone (let the number ring till someone answers—Danes have used an electronic queuing system for years) and English can be used. You do not tip theatre or cinema attendants.

Denmark possesses also a fair number of what for lack of a better English word must be called 'funfairs'. The most famous of course is Copenhagen's Tivoli, described in our 'What to See' section. Simpler pleasures than Tivoli provides can be enjoyed at Bakken just north of central Copenhagen. Tivoli is open from May 1st to the 3rd Sunday in September, and Bakken from mid-April to August 31st. Other towns have entertainment parks inspired by Tivoli and Bakken, and if you visit any of these spots you will not only enjoy yourself—you will also find out a lot about the essential simplicity of the Danish character.

Circus flourishes from April to September at its permanent home in Copenhagen.

Danish museums deserve a little special attention. Apart from the big, 'official' collections of art and antiquities such as you expect in any civilised country, there are also innumerable local museums and tiny private collections on view to the public. It was a Dane who said that every self-respecting town and village expects to have at least one museum. Many of these are extremely informative and others, like Ærøskøbing's private *Bottle-Ship and Pipe Collection* (Flaskeskibs-og Pibe Samling), absorbing and very revealing of the collecting mania that most Danes seem to be born with. Not all private museums are small. Of five notable open-air museums—at Lyngby (near Copenhagen), Odense, Aarhus, Haderslev, and Hjerl Hede—the last is a completely private effort.

Food

Though different, the food served in Danish restaurants is not likely to cause problems for anyone used to British or North American cooking. Cooked dishes include mainly grills, roasts, stews, and so on, served with a considerable variety of fresh vegetables. Given the high quality of the meat and the freshness and variety of the fish available in Denmark it is hardly surprising that most visitors enjoy Danish meals tremendously.

A number of typically Danish dishes are available—a soup, for example, made largely with beer and brown bread; a bacon omelette served in the frying pan; crackly saddle of pork served with sweet red cabbage; fried eel; pickled pork with potatoes and kale; and a number of desserts that use pastries, lightly whipped cream, and fruit.

One particular delicacy—Bornholm smoked herring—should ideally be eaten the moment it comes out of the island smokery. Anyone who enjoys good food will rave over it. The flesh is so succulent and soft that you do not so much eat the herring as drink it.

Chefs and housewives love to display their inventiveness in the *smørrebrød* they prepare, and many open sandwiches are indeed delicious. When eating *smørrebrød* the Danes tend to start with fish and savouries, and then go on to meat and sweet things. But there is no hard and fast rule.

Breakfast in Denmark normally consists of a sizeable pot of tea or coffee, 3 or 4 types of roll or bread, served with butter, and usually also a Danish pastry. Things like cereals and bacon and egg are almost always available as extras. Lunch is served earlier than in most countries—12.00 is a normal time and many restaurants have it available from 11.00 on. When working many Danes eat just a few open sandwiches with a glass of milk for lunch. Dinner starts at 18.00 and in many restaurants goes on being served right up to midnight or later. At home the Danes usually eat early and have coffee with a cake or other snack later in the evening. Your first contact with the Danes at home may well be an invitation to this coffee session.

If possible, avoid taking full board in any but the cheapest hotels and inns. Meals served even in ordinary restaurants tend to be enormous: in good hotels they are even bigger, and it just is not possible to go on eating two of them every day for a week or fortnight.

Drink

The commonest drinks in Denmark are coffee, tea, and milk. Coffee is served very strong and is usually very good, though not cheap. However, you should be warned that Danish coffee has a distinctive flavour of its own which not everyone appreciates. If you ask simply for 'tea' you will be given an English-style pot with a jug of milk.

A tremendous variety of lager beers can be had in Denmark. The Tuborg and Carlsberg brews are already well known in Britain, but you will find a considerable number of other breweries' products very palatable as you travel round Denmark. Draught is available in a number of places, and if you are driving you can always ask for a 'light beer' *(lys øl)*, which tastes like beer but is alcohol-free. (See p 28).

Apart from their beers the Danes' most characteristic drink is called officially *akvavit* (from the latin Aqua Vitae—'water of life') or *snaps*. It is a pretty potent and very pleasant spirit which you swallow at least half a glass at a time. It tastes horrid if you sip it. Cold beer is normally drunk as a chaser between gulps of akvavit.

Something of a ritual usually accompanies the drinking of *snaps*. When your host raises his glass and says *skaal* you must do the same. You then usually clink glasses with everyone present, take a good gulp from your glass, and raise your eyes and your glass again to the others before returning your glass to the table.

Apart from *snaps* Denmark produces a speciality of its own, called *Solbær Rom* (Blackcurrant Rum). A sweet cherry brandy, made by the Heering distillery and called Cherry Heering is also very popular. Both Heering and CLOC manufacture a number of other liqueurs as well as their own whisky and gin. Imported spirits, like imported wines, are heavily taxed and therefore very expensive, particularly when drunk in bars. Despite that they are becoming increasingly popular.

Coca-Cola and other soft drinks can be bought in all restaurants and snack bars, as well as at kiosks in tourist spots.

What to see

It is only in recent years that ordinary foreign holidaymakers have begun to appreciate fully what Denmark offers. While none of the hills are of any great height, the landscapes almost everywhere lack the flatness usually attributed to Denmark. Many areas, such as southern Funen, the east Jutland coast, the Rebild Hills, and parts of Bornholm island have slopes that the most energetic cyclist or walker will find provide an adequate day's exercise. And the cliffs on Møn and Bornholm islands and on the Stevn peninsula are striking enough as scenery for anyone's taste.

But whatever you start by looking for in Denmark, you usually end by enjoying the countryside's extraordinary peacefulness, the liveliness and attractiveness of the towns, and the sheer friendliness and helpfulness of almost everyone you meet. You can drive peacefully on most second-tier main roads, and if you set out to get away from it all you can cycle all day and see only half a dozen motor vehicles. Industry came relatively late to Denmark, and when it arrived the Danes had already learnt to make even industrial towns attractive. There are not many countries where 'Gasworks Avenue' turns out to be one of the best addresses in town—but it happens in Denmark. In this country too you can rely on virtually everyone being ready to give you a hand when you need it, whether he is paid to do so or not.

Every first-time visitor to Denmark will want to see Copenhagen. It is indeed one of Europe's most delightful cities. But, as happens with most capitals, you do not really get to know either the country or its people unless you get out into the villages and smaller towns and the remoter spots. Thanks to Denmark's excellent roads, transport services, and innumerable ferries this is very easy.

Copenhagen

Even before World War II Denmark's capital city enjoyed a well deserved reputation for liveliness, gaiety, colour, and good taste—and recent years have enhanced it. During long summer days, when the sun seems hardly to set at all, its palaces and gardens, colourful old buildings, elegant shops, and bustling seafront make it a wonderful centre for holidaymakers. And even on grey, possibly cold, winter days, when daylight lasts only a few hours, life continues as gay as ever in the city's lively restaurants and nightspots, its bars and theatres and shops. But you must not get the idea that Copenhageners think of nothing but pleasure. One of the city's most extraordinary aspects is that its inhabitants work at least as hard as they play.

Copenhagen today is a bustling modern city. Including adjacent suburbs that are legally separate communities, it is the home of over 1½ million people, more than a quarter of Denmark's entire population. The suburbs' beautifully-designed houses and flats, gay in summer with flowers on windowsills as well as in gardens, are particularly striking, and so are many of the modern office blocks and hotels. But the relatively tiny centre still boasts many enchanting old buildings—sometimes whole streets of them—and winding narrow thoroughfares. Straddling a strait between the larger island of Zealand (Sjælland) and smaller Amager it has the sea right in its heart. And that gives the town a very special atmosphere.

If you want to enjoy the town fully you must do it on foot or by bicycle. Taxi or organised coach tours give a quick glimpse of its main items, but using your own car is not advisable because of one-way streets, and parking problems.

Favourite son: Hans Christian Andersen

The Central Station *(Hovedbanegaard)* makes a good starting point. Its buildings include the Danish Tourist Board's information office (on the right, near the station's Vesterbrogade entrance), the city's Accommodation Bureau (Kiosk P, main booking hall), and a famous restaurant which provides Denmark's (and probably the world's) best Danish 'cold table'.

Opposite the station's Vesterbrogade ('West Bridge Street') exit a column in the middle of the road commemorates the abolition of villeinage in 1788. Turn left down the road and you will come to more modern emancipation in one of the turnings in the form of a riotous collection of sex shops, porn shops, and tarts for every type and taste. In the opposite direction, on the further side from the railway, you come soon to one of Europe's most delightful shops. Called *Den Permanente* (short for 'The Permanent Exhibition of Arts and Crafts'), it is a sort of designers' retail outlet. All products are eligible provided they satisfy an expert selection committee: many of Denmark's most famous firms, such as silversmith Georg Jensen and Royal Copenhagen Porcelain, exhibit there though they have their own shops for sales.

Further on, on Vesterbrogade's other side, you reach the world-famous Tivoli Gardens' main entrance. Laid out beside a selection of the old city moat in 1843 Tivoli has grown into a sort of summary of the entire Danish character. The gardens themselves are beautiful. They contain elegant and exotic and fanciful buildings, all of them very colourful. Entertainments range from a big dipper to a famous marionette theatre, from riotous music hall shows to top-class ballet programmes, symphony concerts and chamber music. You can eat at hot dog *(pølser)* stalls or some of Copenhagen's best and most elegant restaurants.

There is a children's playground, dancing, and community singing— or you can just sit and admire the flowers and the lights. The Tivoli Boy Guards, modelled on the Royal Guard, and their highly skilled band perform on Saturday and Sunday evenings. Firework nights (Wed 23.15, Sat and Sun 23.45) are magnificent. Only Denmark could revel in such a mixture of simplicity and sophistication. Admission varies according to time and day of week, but thousands of Copenhageners buy season tickets: the gardens are open May 1st to the 3rd Sunday in September.

A few seconds' more walk along Vesterbrogade brings you into Town Hall Square *(Raadhuspladsen)*, the city's busiest traffic centre. You can go round the extremely handsome Town Hall, completed in 1905. Apart from elegant staircases, frescoes, painting, and statuary, it contains a remarkable astronomical clock which started working in 1955. It tells the time by various methods, and gives moon phases, star movements, the dates of Easter and other 'movable' Christian feasts—and even incorporates a calendar valid for the next 500,000 years.

A hotel, offices, shops, restaurants, bars, and even an English-style pub are scattered round the square. And opposite Vesterbrogade a string of northward-leading narrow streets, now closed to traffic and known collectively as *Strøget* ('The Strip'), constitutes a major and much loved centre of Copenhagen life. This is the heart of the old town. Some of its houses date back several centuries. Strøget's sides are lined with jostling cinemas, bars, souvenir markets, and elegant shops—Georg Jensen, Bing & Grøndahl, and Royal Copenhagen Porcelain for instance. It passes through the adjacent Gammeltorv and Nytorv Squares (Old Market and New Market), flanks the Church of the Holy Ghost (14th century, rebuilt 1720), with its simple monument to an unknown Danish concentration camp victim, and after a kilometre deposits you in Kongens Nytorv (King's New Square—it is actually circular).

Across the square the Royal Theatre, three theatres in one, is the home of Denmark's Royal Ballet as well as its national theatre company. The Danish Royal Ballet is Western Europe's oldest and one of its best: the earliest item in its repertory dates from 1786. Beside the Royal Theatre the impressive 17th-century mansion called Charlottenborg houses the Royal Academy of Arts. And just beyond it you find the street and waterway called Nyhavn (New Harbour). Once a rowdy seamen's quarter it has become respectable, but still lively, in recent years. It includes some good restaurants, bars, and shops.

Nyhavn is a genuine part of the city's old harbour area. North of it, Amaliegade leads you to the charming rococo royal palace of Amalienborg (built 1754-60). It consists of four identical houses, originally intended for aristocratic families, arranged round a square, and is normally the royal family's summer home. In the little park north of Amalienborg you will see the English-looking church spire projecting above the trees which belongs to St Alban's English church. The double-moated fort beyond it that once guarded the harbour has now been handed over to squatters of all ages in a unique social experiment.

Beyond the fort's main entrance and the ornate Gefion fountain (1907) you reach the sea at the lovely Langelinie Promenade. Here you find colourful restaurants, the Royal Danish Yacht Club, and, perched on a boulder, the famous Little Mermaid (Den lille Havfrue) of Hans Andersen's story, forever looking across the sea to the shipyards on the further island of Amager.

A left turn off Strøget at Gammeltorv takes us to the university quarter, with its bookshops, antique dealers, and boutiques

(Studiestræde and Fiolstræde), and the Regensen student hostel originally built by Christian IV with his observatory Round Tower (*Rundetaarn*) opposite it in Krystalgade. Peter the Great of Russia rode his horse up the tower's internal ramp, intended for heavy astronomical equipment.

Christian IV also designed and built Holy Trinity Church (Trinitatis Kirke) behind the tower and the charming renaissance mansion called Rosenborg a few hundred metres north where he died in 1648. In his day it was a country house outside the city's ramparts. Now, surrounded by Kongens Have ('King's Garden') it houses the Crown Jewels and a museum of royal relics. Off Skindergade, near Regensen, you will find Graabrødretorv (Greyfriars Square), lined with delightful, bright-hued 16th-17th century houses.

A right turn off Strøget at the end of Amagertorv brings you through Højbroplads to Gammelstrand (Old Beach: some good restaurants here), with Slotsholmen (The Castle Island) reached by a bridge across the sea canal. Slotsholm contains Christiansborg Castle, the Thorvaldsen Museum, the Royal Library, the Armoury Museum (Tøjhusmuseet), the highly decorative Stock Exchange designed and built by Christian IV (how did he come to think up the spire of twisted dragons' tails?), and the elegant little naval

Copenhagen: the spire of the Stock Exchange in the foreground, with the Christiansborg Palace immediately behind

Holmens Kirke (The Island's Church), converted from an anchor forge by the architect-king. Modern (1916) despite its appearance, Christiansborg houses the Danish Parliament (Folketing), numerous ministries, and the powerful Ombudsmand's unpretentious office, open to any complainant without even an appointment, beside the Folketing. Traces of Copenhagen's earliest building, the castle raised by Bishop Absalon 800 years ago, can also be seen in Christiansborg (apply main entrance).

With its varied buildings and charming gardens Slotsholmen can easily occupy a day's sightseeing. You could spend a further week in the National Museum beyond the canal just south of Christiansborg. Its collections cover the whole world.

Other specially notable museums and art galleries include the Ny Carlsberg Glyptotek (near the Central Station), northern Europe's finest collection of sculpture of all ages; the State Art Museum (Statens Kunstmuseum, near Rosenborg), a big general collection of paintings and drawings; the Museum of Applied Art (Kunstindustri Museum: near Amalienborg); and the Hirschsprung Gallery of paintings by Danish artists, bequeathed to the city in 1902 (near the State Art Museum).

South of the city centre you can visit the famous Carlsberg Brewery near the Zoo and the large Frederiksberg Have park that has some of Copenhagen's noisiest and liveliest restaurants and nightspots in nearby streets. Westward you reach the very modern Radio Building, Bellahøj hill with its vast trade fair and exhibition building, and the modernistic Grundtvig Church at Bispebjerg, built to honour the founder of the Folk High School movement.

Northward you come, inland, to a string of lakes where you can walk and cycle and make excursions by motorboat, to the charming little 18th-century Sorgenfri (Sans Souci) palace, and the great Frilandsmuseet (Open Air Museum) of re-erected old farms and village houses, started in 1901 and part of the National Museum. Along the coast you pass the Tuborg Brewery (which you can also visit), the vast wooded Charlottenlund park, Klampenborg's fine but very crowded Bellevue beach (Copenhageners call it 'The Fly Paper'), and its Dyrehave (Deer Park), a former royal hunting ground containing Eremitagen (The Hermitage)—originally a hunting lodge, and the well-patronised Bakken amusement park and funfair. You can reach all these places quickly by electric S-train *(S-tog),* but a restful return route from Klampenborg in summer is by motorboat.

Motorboat ferries will also give you a relaxed trip from Nyhavn to the charming old harbour quarter of Christianshavn, which still preserves its canals and moated fortifications alongside the vast

Burmeister & Wain works where half the world's merchant navy
marine diesels are made and the baroque Vor Frelsers Kirke
(Church of Our Saviour), with its elegant gilded spiral-staircase
spire (which you can climb). Beyond Christianshavn lies the rest of
Amager island, with Copenhagen's modern airport at Kastrup, the

Bakken: the largest amusement park in northern Europe

Amager Museum at Store Magleby where many Dutchmen settled
in the 16th century, and a ferry port with fast links to Malmö in
Sweden at Dragør.

Ferries cross from Havnegade to Malmö in Sweden ($1\frac{1}{2}$ hrs), from
Dragør to Limhavn near Malmø (50 min), and from Tuborg
Harbour to Landskrona, midway between Malmö and Hälsingborg
($1\frac{1}{4}$ hrs). There are less frequent services to Travemünde in West
Germany (8-9 hours) and Oslo in Norway (16 hours).

Aabenraa

A pleasant small port town about 20 km north of the German
frontier on the main road (A10) to North Jutland, Aabenraa lies
at the head of an attractive fjord (the word in Danish means 'bay')
on Jutland's hilly eastern side. It once handled important trade
with Iceland and Baltic ports and is now a flourishing market town.

Aalborg

Denmark's fourth largest town, with a population approaching 100,000 excluding independent suburbs, Aalborg lies about 110 km south of Jutland's northern tip on the southern side of a branch of the Limfjord (see Mors) which cuts right through Northern Jutland, linking the North Sea to the Baltic. Noted mainly for its cement and tobacco manufactures and for its production of aquavit—Danes often use the term 'Aalborg' as an alternative to *snaps*—Aalborg is also an attractive holiday base with a delightful old centre.

This central area has been made into a traffic-free precinct. Its focal point is the delightful brick-built Gothic Cathedral, dating mainly from about 1500 in its present form and dedicated to the English seamen's patron saint St Botolph. In Danish its name is Budolfi Kirke, and like all Danish churches its interior is colourful enough to surprise British and American visitors. Unusual wooden galleries line each side of the nave: the paintings on their panels include the arms of Christian VII of Denmark and the royal coat of arms of England: Christian's wife was an English princess. The pulpit is brightly coloured, as in most Danish churches. Some decorated pew ends date from 1739: others are more recent.

In Gammel Torv (Old Market) north of the Cathedral the town's delightful small Town Hall, little changed since it was built in 1762, stands in the north-east corner. Visitors are sometimes admitted: the baroque meeting-rooms upstairs are charming. In Budolfi Plads (St Botolph's Square) to the south the Aalborg Museum lies west of the Cathedral immediately beyond the fine Post Office building (with dovecots thoughtfully provided for the pigeons that were bound to settle there anyway). Along with an art collection the museum concentrates on local life and history, including important Viking relics.

The Monastery of the Holy Ghost (Helligaandsklostret) in C.W.Obels Plads behind the Post Office admits visitors to its delightful chapter house, refectory, and cellars. Built in 1432 to house monks and nuns and 60 ill or elderly people, it is Denmark's oldest publicly supported charity.

In Østeraagade (just beyond the Town Hall: turn left) two fine old merchants' houses have been carefully preserved. The first, Jens Bangs Stenhus (Jens Bang's Brick House), is a magnificent 6-storey mansion dating from 1624, when bricks were still rare and luxurious. Jørgen Olufsens Gaard, a little further on, was timber-frame-built in 1616. Further down the road you reach the Aalborghus, a former royal castle overlooking the harbour and still used as an administrative centre: visitors are allowed into the charming 16th-century half-timbered courtyard.

The Tingbæk chalkmines, 26 km south of Aalborg

In Vesterbro, parallel with Østeraagade west of the Budolfi Plads pedestrian precinct (you can reach it through Bispensgade, the town's main shopping centre), two fine groups of statuary typify the Danes' love of beauty and their readiness to spend public money on achieving it. Near the harbour the 'Cimbrian Bull', by Anders Bundgaard, recalls the Danish tribe from the nearby Himmerland region. Inland, the Goose Girl, by Gerhard Henning, is even more famous.

Further inland still you come to the impressive Aalborghallen (The Aalborg Hall), dating from 1949. Aalborghallen contains over 800 rooms. The main assembly hall holds 3,400 people and can cope with anything from chamber music to a full-scale circus. Visitors can see over the complex when not in use.

Beyond the Aalborg Hall a series of parks includes the Møllepark and its zoo (some good restaurants in this area). Beyond them you come to Karolinelund, Aalborg's version of Copenhagen's Tivoli (see p 40). Algade and its continuations, running eastward from the Cathedral, contain a number of modest old one and two-storeyed timbered houses. In Nørresundby on the harbour's northern side, reached by a modern bridge, you find the vast Lindholm Høje Viking burial ground. It includes 140 'ship graves', tombs enclosed by standing stones making the outline shape of a boat.

46

Aarhus

Denmark's second city, her second busiest port (surpassed only by Esbjerg), large producer of beer, locomotives, vegetable oils, and refrigerators, university city and seat of a bishopric for over 1000 years, Aarhus is also an important holiday centre. It has fine parks, 15 km of excellent beaches north and south of the town, numerous hotels, restaurants, and nightspots, and an old city centre almost as charming as Aalborg's. In Denmark you have to accustom yourself to the idea that industrial cities can be also very beautiful. A lively Festival Week (early Sep) covers arts, sports, shops, street entertainers—everything.

The old town's centre is the Store Torv (Great Square), only a stone's throw from the harbour. The streets are winding and narrow here. A belt developed mainly in the 19th century surrounds this area. A by-pass road, part of the town's 20th-century planning, runs outside this region, about $1\frac{1}{2}$ km from the Cathedral. Parks and cliffs at the by-pass's two ends and the hills and parks that flank it provide a very attractive layout.

On top of slopes dropping steeply to the shore north of the town the Risskov (or Riisskov: *skov*=wood) provides grazing for herds of deer under its beechwoods. Humans who go to stroll there can eat and drink well in the famous Sjette Frederiks Kro (Frederik VI Inn). Immediately below the slopes two enclosed bathing establishments, reserved for nude bathers, have been operating for generations. No one bothers that you can see into them from above: the car park is an ideal vantage point.

About $1\frac{1}{2}$ km from the Frederik VI Inn the by-pass Ring Road (Ringgade) runs beside the University which was founded in 1928 and boasts many excellent modern buildings spread over the green hills. Another kilometre brings you to the Botanical Gardens, laid out as a public park on the slope of another hill. At the bottom of the Gardens, on the town-centre (NE) side, you can walk without payment or formality into the charming open-air museum called Den gamle By (The Old Town: main entrance in Viborgvej). The Old Town consists of a delightful collection of genuine old houses re-erected to form an old town, with cobbled streets and a stream flowing through the middle. You can go into a number of buildings, filled with items typical of particular trades.

A whole complex of parks stretches along the hills and cliffs south of the town. First comes Friheden with its zoo, nature trail, sports complex, and observatory. Then the Mindepark (Memorial Park), dedicated to Danes who died in World War I. From the Mindepark you can see Marselisborg Palace inland: it was given to King Christian X (1912-1947) by the people of Denmark and the public are not admitted. Marselisborg Skov and Storskov stretch for 8 km beyond the Mindepark. Here and on the beach, where the bathing is excellent, there are a number of pleasant restaurants.

In the town's old centre the main places of interest are the late-Gothic 15th-century brick-built Cathedral, the 12th-century Vor Frue Kirke (Church of Our Lady), Aarhus's oldest building and the town's original Cathedral, and the Aarhus Museum of art and antiquities. The 'Grauballe Man', one of several accidentally mummified bodies discovered in Jutland bogs, can be seen in the Moesgaard Museum. They are believed to have been the voluntary victims of ritual sacrifices in the early centuries of the Christian era.

Just south of the old town centre Aarhus's impressive and very modern Town Hall (Raadhus) was one of the first buildings to make the name of the now world-famous architect-designer Arne Jacobsen. It was completed in 1942. Visitors are taken round in groups at fixed hours. The town's Tourist Office stands beside the Town Hall.

Ærøskøbing and Ærø island

Ærø island lies due south of Funen and its chief town and port, Ærøskøbing, is reached by ferry from Svendborg (see separate entry) in 1¼ hours.

Ærøskøbing

Ærøskøbing is widely appreciated as the most perfectly preserved of all Denmark's tiny old towns. Little more than a village in size its streets are still cobbled and lined with lovely, brightly-painted, tiny 17th-18th century timber-frame houses, gay with flowers in summer. We owe this little gem's continued existence mainly to Gunnar Hammerich, a sculptor who went to live in Ærøskøbing in 1916 and fought long and hard for its preservation. Astonishingly enough, he still lives there, and runs a delightful small museum in his own little house, called Hammerichs Hus.

Another little private museum, called in Danish Flaskeskibs-og Pibe Samling (usually translated as 'Bottle-Ship and Pipe Collection'), is perhaps more popular: it consists of hundreds of model ships in bottles and pipes from all over the world. But Ærøskøbing's real delight is simply strolling through its ancient, peaceful streets or sailing a yacht into its delightful small harbour.

A single main road runs Ærø island's whole length (about 25km), through the villages that cluster on its central ridge. The pleasant rolling landscape is dotted with windmills. Marstal village, at Ærø's eastern end, still has a number of old houses. In the years before steam it was an important seafaring and shipbuilding centre. Its Maritime Museum recalls those days, and also displays a number of Stone Age grinding troughs and spherical grinding stones, all found locally, that are between 8,000 and 10,000 years old. A ferry connects Marstal to Rudkøbing on Langeland island in 1 hour (see Langeland).

Als island See Sønderborg.

Billund

If it seems strange that a Central Jutland village of 2000 inhabitants, 28 km west of Vejle, should have an airport capable of taking the world's largest jets, a 1st-class hotel, and an outstandingly good campsite, the reasons are not far to seek. The airport was built largely to handle worldwide charter air traffic for Europe's largest travel firm, built up in his spare time by Pastor Eilif Kroager, parish priest of Tjæreborg village near Esbjerg. The hotel and campsite cope with visitors to the vast entertainment centre called Legoland (pronounced Lee-golan in Danish).

The world-famous constructional toy Lego, today manufactured under licence in some 60 countries, was invented by the village carpenter's son in Billund. Now a millionaire he continues, like the Tjæreborg priest, to live in his village. But he has had Legoland built on a 25-acre site.

Centred on a charming model village designed in differing styles by a team of architects, who used 20 million Lego bricks to build it, Legoland includes also a superb doll museum, a Wild West riding centre, a children's road safety training course (which is great fun: you have to obey all the road signs correctly), and much else. A million people visited Legoland in its first 8 months, though the model village seems to interest old age pensioners more than children.

Legoland

Bornholm island

Nearly 200 km eastward journey by boat from Copenhagen, Bornholm lies within sight of southern Sweden. Its landscapes of tall granite cliffs and rocky coasts, sloping down to miles of silvery sand at Dueodde in the south, is as untypical of Denmark as anything could be. But its inhabitants have more than once shown themselves passionately Danish in character and outlook.

Bornholm (accent on the second syllable) is famous for its strangely clear light, its delicious smoked herrings, its often wild scenery, its brightly coloured farmhouses and other old buildings, its 4 ancient circular churches (built for defence against Wendish pirates, like two others in Denmark and a number in southern Sweden), and its minute harbours that were once filled with fishing craft and are now extremely popular with Danish and other yachtsmen. Bornholm is one of Denmark's main holiday areas.

The very comfortable and surprisingly cheap ferries from Copenhagen deposit you in Rønne, the capital and chief port, after a 7-hour journey (nightly all year, daily also in summer). You can also fly there in half an hour.

Rønne has whole streets of colourful small houses near the Store Torv (Great Market), its old town centre. On the island's east coast the harbour towns of Neksø, Svaneke, Tejn and, in particular, Gudhjem all have clusters of centuries-old small timbered houses. Bright colourings are traditional, with sandstone red and black predominating, but greens, yellows, blues and every imaginable hue are also now popular. Tejn is noteworthy as being the smallest of all the harbours.

Bornholm's scenery is at its wildest at Hammeren (The Hammer) at its northern tip. The cliffs here rise 75 metres above the sea. Surrounded by heather-covered slopes, which offer very pleasant walking, the gaunt ruins of Hammershus, a 13th-century fortress, look out towards Sweden. There are craggy cliffs at Helligdommen, north of Gudhjem on the eastern coast, and at Jons Kapel (John's Chapel: named after a hermit who used to preach there) south of Hammershus. Inland, the wooded Paradisbakkerne (Hills of Paradise), 3—5 km from the coast between Neksø and Svaneke, and the wooded, hilly Almindingen area at the island's centre are delightful to explore, especially on foot.

The four circular churches, originally defence towers, at Olsker (pronounced Oles-kor), Nyker (Nü-kor), Østerlars, and Nylars have each their own character. The church at Aakirkeby was also originally fortified and has a magnificently coloured and carved wooden pulpit.

Allinge and Sandvig, on the east coast just south of Hammeren, are the main holiday centres. But accommodation of every sort, including well-built chalets, is available in every part of the island. There are sandy beaches large and small scattered right round the coast—or you can dive into 3 or 6 metres of clear water from low rocks.

The island of Bornholm, 8 hours' voyage from Copenhagen

Ebeltoft

A market town since 1301 Ebeltoft still preserves its narrow, cobbled streets and a considerable number of small half-timbered, brightly coloured houses. One of them, built in 1576, used to be the Town Hall and is now a museum. The old Dyer's House (Farvergaarden) and Post House (Postgaarden) also house museum collections. Ebeltoft has a fine sandy beach in a well-sheltered bay on the further side of the Mols peninsula from Aarhus. With good hotels and other accommodation, including chalets, it is a holiday area very popular with Danes and others. The road distance from Aarhus is 47 km. A fast, comfortable ferry, connecting Ebeltoft to Sjællands Odde (see North Zealand) in 1½ hours with up to 18 sailings a day, provides a quick car route to Copenhagen and intermediate towns.

Esbjerg

Built to handle Danish exports to Britain just over a century ago, Esbjerg is the arrival port for comfortable and fast DFDS ferries from Harwich and Newcastle. Completely modern—only 20 people lived there in 1868—it is an extraordinarily clean and neat port. The town, too, is attractively laid out and has become increasingly industrial in recent years. Its attractions include a good municipal Art Gallery specialising in modern art and a seawater aquarium.

Esbjerg is the obvious starting-point for car tours of Denmark. It has good accommodation and restaurants. The ferry excursion to Fanø island (20 minutes: see separate entry), and perhaps a visit to the 320 km sandy beach that starts immediately north, are well worth while.

Faaborg

Faaborg is a pleasant small port and yachting centre 40 km south of Odense. A number of attractive narrow streets and mainly 18th-century small timbered houses have survived, and there is a small art gallery devoted to the works of painters born on Funen island. Ferries operate from Faaborg to the tiny Danish islands of Avernakø and Lyø (½ hour), to Gelting in Germany (2¼ hours), and to Søby near Ærø's western tip (1 hour). From Bøjden, 12 km west of Faaborg, you can cross to Fynshav on Als island (see Sønderborg), connected by a bridge to southern Jutland.

Faaborg, on the island of Funen

Falster island

Falster has Zealand and Møn to its north, Lolland on its west.
Coming from Copenhagen you cross from Vordingborg on Zealand
to the island's north coast by the vast Storstrøm road and rail
bridge (Storstrømbroen), 3 km long, built by a British firm in 1937.
From Lolland separate road and rail bridges cross the narrow
Guldborg Sound separating the islands.

Falster's main towns are Stubbekøbing and Nykøbing (Nykøbing
Falster to distinguish it from other Nykøbings). Falster is mainly
flat, but has pleasant scenery round much of its coast, with a really
magnificent long sandy beach down the eastern side of its southern
tip. The beach takes its name from the minute village of Bøtø By
(Bøtø Town). Europe's cheapest car ferry, run by Danish Railways,
operates from Gedser, at Falster's southernmost point, to
Warnemünde in East Germany: a car up to 6 m and driver costs
only 69 kr return (about £5.50) for the 2-hour journey. Another
ferry connects Gedser to Travemünde in West Germany (3 hours).

Fanø island

Some 15 km long, lying off the west Jutland coast opposite Esbjerg,
Fanø has long been a popular bathing and holiday resort. Its main
attraction is the vast sandy beach down its western edge, wide
enough to serve also as a summer road, complete with speed limit
signs. The ferry from Esbjerg (20 minutes: departures every half-
hour) lands visitors at Nordby village. Sønderho in the south has a
number of old houses, including an attractive old inn, dating from
sailing ship days, when Sønderho and Fanø were important
shipping centres. 'Family'-standard hotels, flats, chalet and campsite
accommodation are available.

Fredericia

You pronounce the town's name Frederitsia or Fredereechia
according to what part of Denmark you come from. Roughly
100 km from Esbjerg and 55 from Odense, Fredericia was built on a
peninsula in 1650 by Frederik III (hence its name) to guard the
Little Belt (Lille Bælt) strait between Jutland and Funen. The earth
rampart hastily thrown up by thousands of Jutland peasants on the
landward side is still almost intact. The streets were laid out in grid
pattern to enable cannon on the ramparts to fire also at attackers
landing on the shore.

Good bathing is possible at Snoghøj just south of the town. Hotels
become specially full in early August, during Fredericia's annual
Trade Fair.

Funen (Fyn) island

Funen (Fyn in Danish) is the large island centrally placed between Jutland and Zealand. It is connected to Jutland by the Little Belt bridges, to Zealand by rail and car ferries across the Great Belt, to Taasinge and Langeland islands by bridges, and to Germany, and Als and other smaller islands by ferries from Assens (in the west), Bøjden, Faaborg, and Svendborg.

Funen's capital, Odense, and the main centres of Faaborg, Nyborg, and Svendborg are described separately. To Danes Funen is 'the Garden of Denmark'—justifiably so, since flowers abound. The Svanninge Hills in the south, inland from Faaborg and Svendborg, are jokingly called 'the Funen Alps'. Though not very high, their wooded slopes provide lovely views and attractive walks and cycle rides. North-east of Odense (about 18 km) a special museum has been built at Ladby to house the famous Viking burial-ship excavated there in 1935 (follow the signs saying 'Ladby Skibet'). The chieftain buried in it 1000 years ago took with him to Valhalla his arms and armour, 4 hunting dogs, and 11 horses. At Nørre Lyndelse (about 15 km south of Odense) you can see the village musician's home where the great Danish composer Carl Nielsen (1865-1931) was born.

But perhaps the greatest of all Funen's glories is its many fine manor houses, concentrated most thickly in the island's south and west but found everywhere. The most notable of them, Egeskov (near Kværndrup, some 32 km south of Odense), is a superb Renaissance moated castle, surrounded by its original moat and by five gardens in different styles, including a reconstruction of the one laid out when the great house was built.

Egeskov has a direct connection with Shakespeare's *Hamlet* that the 'castle of Elsinore' (see Helsingør) lacks. In 1599 an unmarried daughter of the house, Rigborg Brockenhuus, was found to be pregnant and was sentenced by the king to be imprisoned in her room in Egeskov for the rest of her father's life—happily he lived only 5 more years. The father of the illegitimate child was Frederik Rosenkrantz, recently returned with his friend Guldenstjerne (which is how old Danish records spell the name) from service with the Danish ambassador at the court of St James's, where he must surely have become known to Shakespeare.

Egeskov is outstanding by any standards. But the other manor houses are all worth seeing. Some are open to the public at certain times: others, like Egeskov, open only their gardens, and some can only be glimpsed from the road. The Odense Tourist Office can provide detailed and up-to-date information. We cannot unfortunately list details, but their names are:

Egeskov

Ulriksholm, Gyldensten, Margaard, Langesø (north of Odense), Juulskov, Holckenhavn, Ravnholt, Ørbæklunde, Lykkesholm, Glorup, Hesselagergaard, Hvidkilde, Rygaard, Nakkebølle, Broholm, Mullerup, Holstenhus, Brahetrolleborg, Brahesborg, and Arreskov (to the south).

Charming old manor houses can be found all over Denmark, but Funen's are conveniently thickly clustered.

Grenaa

Now 3 km from the sea the pleasant old town of Grenaa was once a busy port at the mouth of the Green River (Gren Aa) on the Djurs peninsula projecting east into the Kattegat at Jutland's widest point. Randers lies 55 km west and Viborg 96. Ferries connect Grenaa's new harbour with Hundested on Zealand and with Anholt island in the middle of the Kattegat.

Haderslev

Haderslev straddles a narrow, winding fjord on Jutland's hilly east side, 24 km north of Aabenraa and 46 from the German frontier by highway A10. The chief points of interest are the mainly 15th-century Gothic Cathedral and the 'Latin School' founded in 1567 beside it. Accommodation is available.

Helsingør (Elsinore)

Since the 12th century there has been a castle at Helsingør, barely 4 km from the Swedish coast on the Øresund's other side. For over 400 years, up to 1857, the Danish kings acquired a fair proportion of their income by levying charges on shipping passing through the strait: the North European maritime nations bought them out with a down payment of £4 million. When Shakespeare wrote *Hamlet* English seamen were thoroughly familiar with Helsingør, which they called Elsinore, but Kronborg castle there never had any direct connection with Hamlet, who was a Prince of Jutland.

Kronborg in its present imposing form was built by Dutch architects for Frederik II in 1547, and rebuilt with alterations by Christian IV after a disastrous fire in 1629. You enter through a gate in the formidable outer ramparts and cross part of the old moat by a bridge. Rooms open to the public include the Guardroom; the State Apartments (including rooms first furnished

Kronborg Castle in Elsinore.

for James VI of Scotland, later James I of England, after his marriage to Anne of Denmark in 1589); Christian IV's dining room containing 7 of the original tapestries representing Danish kings, woven at Helsingør by Flemish weavers in 1584; the Chapel which, unlike everything mentioned above, has retained its original appearance instead of the altered image provided by Christian IV; the Telegraph Tower, which provides a good view of the Sound and the Swedish coast; and the kitchens and casements, where you will see a statue of the mythical Holger Danske (Ogier the Dane), a sort of King Arthur figure who will reputedly waken and come to Denmark's aid if ever the country is in desperate straits.

The former Carmelite Monastery (Karmeliterklostret) off Havnegade just inland from the castle has survived in its original Gothic style. You can visit the refectory, chapter house, and chapel. The great organ composer Buxtehude, probably born at Hälsingborg on the Sound's Swedish side, was organist at the monastery from 1660 to 1667. The 16th-17th century English lutenist John Dowland dated some of his compositions from Helsingør.

Helsingør is also famous for its International People's College, founded in 1921 to promote international understanding.

Copenhagen is about 50 km away. Frequent ferries cross to Hälsingborg in 20 or 25 minutes.

Herning

Once a village known for its handweaving, Herning is now a sizeable and flourishing modern textile centre whose factories are known for imaginative modern ideas. The Angli factory, in particular, is almost as much art gallery as workplace, so that machine minders and office staff alike enjoy beautiful and frequently changed art displays while they work.

Herning holds a Textile Fair every March. It has a pleasant small museum of local life and history and a fine new circular art gallery. The town lies 35 km west of Silkeborg by road and 77 km from Aarhus.

Holstebro

The little town of Holstebro (population 33,000) is an important west Jutland communications centre. Though ancient, its old buildings have all been destroyed by disastrous fires. And though small it is a town where all the arts—theatre, music, sculpture and everything else—flourish to an extraordinary degree. Leading orchestras and theatre companies visit the town. A large proportion of its inhabitants play musical instruments. And the Town Council spends the equivalent of about £7 a head each year on supporting these activities. It lies 51 km west of Viborg and 34 north-west of Herning.

Horsens

A sizeable industrial town situated on one of east Jutland's less attractive fjords, 51 km south of Aarhus and 27 north of Vejle by highway A10. Horsens was founded some 900 years ago and was an important fortified town in medieval times. A number of old buildings have survived. The pleasant 18th-century manor house Bygholm Slot, just west of the town, is now a hotel. The church in the little village of Ut (or Uth), about 6 km south-east of the town, has tombs of both the Rosenkrantz and Guldenstjerne families from which Shakespeare's *Hamlet* characters are drawn.

Jelling

A thousand years ago the little village of Jelling was Denmark's Viking capital. Two huge round barrows north and south of the ancient little church have always been regarded as the tombs of King Gorm the Old, first ruler of a united Denmark, and of his Queen, Thyra, the last Danish monarchs to be buried as pagans. Excavations, however, have shown that Gorm's Hill (Gorms Høj), south of the church, contained no burial chamber, while Thyra's Hill once held two bodies—we cannot tell whose.

Two large runic stones found at Jelling and now in the churchyard have been nicknamed 'Denmark's birth certificate' and 'Denmark's first court circular'. The larger, about 2½ m high, makes the first unmistakeable historical reference to Denmark. It was set up in memory of Gorm and Thyra by their son, Harald Bluetooth (Harald Blaatand), 'who won all Denmark and Norway for himself and made the Danes Christians'. It is remarkable for its carving of the crucified Christ embracing the world—Scandinavia's oldest representation of Christ—and for the fact that the runes run horizontally and not vertically, perhaps because the carver came from England. The smaller stone, about 1½ m high, tells us that 'King Gorm raised this monument to the memory of his wife Thyra'.

The little church has several remarkable features. The present building dates in part from the 10th or 11th centuries. But postholes for an earlier wooden church were discovered in 1948—you can see them through plate-glass let into the chancel floor. Specialists are certain that the large stone slab in the chancel, used 900 years ago as the altar, came—somehow—from Greece. Byzantine-style murals were discovered under the chancel's whitewash in 1874. And the church itself is centrally placed in a V of standing stones, almost certainly supplanting an earlier point of pagan worship.

Jelling lies about 14 km north-west of Vejle by the A18 and a kilometre or two more if you travel via the attractively hilly and well wooded Grejs valley *(Grejsdal)*.

Køge

Of all Zealand's old towns Køge alone has retained a really impressive number of old half-timbered houses, mostly from the 16th and 17th centuries. Since it also has two good beaches barely 40 km south of Copenhagen it is naturally a very popular holiday and excursion spot. It is also quite an important manufacturing town.

One of the town's main sights is the Nicolaj Kirke. Its huge fortified tower dates back to the 14th century. Any Wendish pirates who were caught used to be hanged from the tower windows. Hans

Køge

Andersen refers to them by their old name of 'Køge chickens'. The decorated pew ends, pulpit, and altarpiece date from the early 17th century. No. 20 Kirkestræde (Church Street), which leads from St Nicholas' to Torvet (The Market) is reputedly Denmark's oldest house of known date (1527), and other old houses can be seen in streets leading off Torvet. The Town Hall (Raadhus) in Nørregade (North Street) was built in the 16th century but given a new façade in 1803. Another old house in Nørregade houses the Køge Museum. There is of course a main tourist office in Køge.

Køge is a good base from which to explore Stevns, the broad peninsula ending in cliffs, known as Stevns Klint, over 30 m high and 15 km long, between Køge Bay (Køge Bugt) and Fakse Bay. There is good bathing and good scenery in this region.

Kolding

Kolding is another of hilly east Jutland's attractively situated fjord towns. It stands at the point where the A1 Esbjerg-Odense-Copenhagen road crosses the A10 from the German frontier to northern Jutland, some 63 km east of Esbjerg and 70 km west of Odense. Originally a fortress town, it now manufactures textiles, hardware, bacon, chocolate, and much else.

Of the town's old buildings the most important is the Koldinghus, the royal castle built in 1248 to ward off incursions from the south (the present German frontier is 70 km away). Burnt down by an accidental fire in 1808, during the Napoleonic Wars, it has never since been rebuilt, but its ruins provide the town with a picturesque backdrop.

Korsør

Though relatively important as a Zealand manufacturing town some 110 km west of Copenhagen, Korsør is known to visitors mainly as a terminus for the train ferries crossing the Great Belt. The car ferries, nowadays much busier, ply from Halsskov immediately north. Advance car bookings are essential in summer.

Krusaa

This small south Jutland village is the frontier crossing point of the main A10-E3 highway from Germany.

Læsø island

This once-remote island in the Kattegat is famous for its heath-and-dune scenery, its old timbered houses thatched with sea-grass, its pines and birchwoods, and its fine bathing. You reach it by ferry in 1 hour 40 mins from Frederikshavn (see North Jutland).

Langeland island

Langeland, some 55 km long and 10 km at its widest, lies south-west of Funen. You can reach it by road from Svendborg, across bridges connecting Funen to Taasinge island, Taasinge to tiny Siø island, and Siø to Rudkøbing, Langeland's main town. Rudkøbing is also connected to Marstal (see Ærø island) by ferry (1 hour). Lohals, near Langeland's northern tip, has a ferry connection to Korsør (1½ hours). From Spodsberg on the island's eastern side you can reach Nakskov on Lolland island in 1 hour 20 mins. From Bagenkop at the southern tip, ferries ply to Kiel in West Germany in 2 hours 20 mins (up to 3 departures daily in summer).

Rudkøbing is an old port and has been a market town since 1287. Many timbered houses have survived, and its church dates from the 12th century. The town's Langeland Museum has a first-rate collection illustrating the island's history.

In the rest of the island the small settlements are not particularly important. But the scenery is pleasantly hilly and dotted with windmills, for which Langeland is famous, and there are cliffs at Ristinge in the south. The fine moated manor house of Tranekær, about 12 km north of Rudkøbing, has been a royal residence since 1231. There are lesser manors at Stensgaard, Nedergaard, and Egeløkke in the north, and Skovsgaard, Hjortholm, and Broløkke in the south.

There are good bathing beaches at Ristinge and Østerbadet in the south, and at Spodsbjerg, Lohals, and Emmerbølle (near Tranekær, on the west coast). A main tourist office operates at Rudkøbing.

Lolland island

As its name 'Lowland' suggests, most of Lolland is really flat. But there are some attractive corners—notably the manor houses of Søholm (overlooking the large lake south of Maribo), Knuthenborg and its lovely 'English' park about 6 km north of Maribo, and Kristianssæde, about 12 km south-west. Apart from Maribo the main towns are Sakskøbing and Nakskov.

A special sort of attraction, in the form of a really superb veteran car museum, is provided by Aalholm Castle, itself an attractive old manor house near Nysted on the island's south coast, about 30 km from both Maribo and Rødbyhavn. Nysted has a fine beach to its east.

Lolland lies between Langeland and Falster islands. It is connected to the former by the Nakskov-Spodsbjerg ferry (1 hour 20 mins) and to the latter by bridges across the narrow strait. The ferry that comes into the little modern port of Rødbyhavn, on Lolland's south coast, from Puttgarden in West Germany constitutes a major car route into Denmark (crossing 1 hour: up to 28 departures daily in summer).

Møn island

Møn's main feature is the magnificent stretch of high chalk cliffs, known as Møns Klint, at its eastern edge. Running for a good 8 km their maximum height is 128 m. Many of the formations have been eroded into strange shapes, given fanciful names like 'Queen's Chair' and 'Summer Spire'. They are shot with varying colours, covered for much of their extent with massive beechwoods, and cut by ravines which you can clamber down to reach the beach. Lower cliffs continue northwards. Ulvshale, north of Stege, Møn's 'capital', offers good bathing, and churches at Elmelunde, Keldby, and Fanefjord contain very striking 15th-century frescoes of country scenes. Møn is linked to Zealand by a road bridge.

Møn's Cliffs—one of Denmark's outstanding beauty spots

Mors island and the Limfjord

An inland island in a country made up mostly of islands seems odd.
But Mors lies in the middle of the vast and complicated expanse of
water, known as the Limfjord, which cuts right across northern
Jutland. On its western side it is protected against North Sea
flooding by dykes. In the east it provides Aalborg, seemingly inland,
with a deep-sea harbour.

Nykøbing (called Nykøbing Mors to distinguish it from towns of
the same name on Falster and Zealand islands) is Mors's only town.
It is famous chiefly for its oyster beds. A thousand and more years
ago the surrounding Limfjord's shores provided raiding bases for
Vikings. Today, a number of towns stand round it. The most
important are: Skive, Struer, Lemvig, Thisted (or Tisted), and
Løgstør.

Skive is a charming town, beautifully located on a hill sloping down
to the Skive Fjord, an inner inlet off the Limfjord. It is an extremely
popular yachting centre. Though very ancient the church is almost
its only surviving old building. Struer is a purely modern industrial
town, but Lemvig is another ancient settlement with a natural
harbour. Løgstør, now a market town, was once important for its
herring fisheries. Thisted, main town of the narrow strip of land
separating the Limfjord from the North Sea, is the chief settlement
of the region called Thy (pronounced Tü).

North Jutland and the North-West Coast

From Esbjerg northwards, Jutland's entire west coast with its
magnificent wide sandy beach backed by extensive dunes, occasional
cliffs, and sometimes vast lagoons, is a sort of continuous holiday
area in summer. There are relatively few towns apart from the lovely
old settlement of Ringkøbing, on the landward side of the large
Ringkøbing Fjord lagoon, a number on the shores of the extensive
and complex Limfjord (see Mors and the Limfjord), and others
near Jutland's northern tip. Even the villages—Nørre Vorupor,
Klitmøller, Slettestrand, Svinkløv, Hanstholm (noted for its cliffs),
Bulbjerg (also with cliffs), Torupstrand, and the rest are tiny—until
you come to the larger and livelier resort centres of Blokhus and
Løkken, with smaller Lønstrup beyond. Apart from 1st-class hotels
at Hanstholm, Blokhus, and Løkken the main pattern of
holidaymaking is one of family stays in more modest hotels and
pensions, in chalets, and on campsites, with the beach and nature as
holidaymakers' main delights: there are bird sanctuaries among the
lagoons.

Hirtshals and Frederikshavn near Jutland's northern tip are port
towns with ferries operating respectively to Kristiansand (4 hours)

and Arendal (4 hours: both in Norway); and to Larvik in Norway (5 hours) and Oslo (10 hours, summer only), and Gothenburg (Göterborg) in Sweden (3 hours). Hjørring, inland, is a market town noted for its parks. There are good bathing beaches north of Frederikshavn and close to Bangsbo, an 18th-century manor that is now a museum, about 2 km south. On the way north to Skagen you can make a detour about 12 km short of the town to the dunes of Raabjerg Mile, which have been moving slowly eastwards for years.

The town of Skagen, busy fishing port, summer resort, and artists' centre all in one, rather like St Ives in Cornwall, is however the main attraction for visitors in this corner of Denmark. It has restaurants. a number of small hotels, and a small museum of the type you expect in every self-respecting Danish town. Skagen's is housed in old fishermen's cottages and deals largely with the region's seafaring history.

Skagen has been transformed in English into The Skaw. But the English name is mostly applied to the sandy spit of land which forms Jutland's northern extremity, known in Danish as Grenen (The Tip). It is a very unimpressive headland—except that it enables you to stand with one foot in the North Sea and the other in the Kattegat.

North Zealand

Most of the northern part of Zealand (Sjælland) island is outstandingly popular as a holiday resort, not only because it is close to Copenhagen but also because it offers outstandingly pleasant and—off the main roads between Copenhagen and Helsingør—peaceful countryside, a wide choice of hotels and other accommodation, and excellent bathing from large sandy beaches in the extreme north. (The fastest route between Copenhagen and Helsingør is the crowded motorway.)

The coast is built-up almost the whole 30 km from Klampenborg on Copenhagen's northern outskirts to Helsingør (see separate entries), and the road flanking it is mercilessly busy in summer. While the beaches are at best only a few metres wide bathing is by no means impossible, and there are a number of pleasant and comfortable places where you can stay, such as Snekkersten, about 4 km south of Helsingør. Humlebæk, about 5 km south of Snekkersten, boasts the superb Louisiana Museum of Modern Art, where concerts are also given and where you can eat very well in the museum's famous restaurant.

North of Helsingør Marienlyst has a pleasant beach and a famous luxury hotel. Hellebæk, about 5 km further on, can boast an even better beach and another luxury hotel. Hornbæk, 12 km from Helsingør, is a fishing village with old streets and houses lying below wooded hills with magnificent views across the Sound. As you continue round Zealand's northernmost tip you come to a series of ever better and larger beaches at Dronningmølle, Gilleleje (another old fishing village), Raageleje, Tisvildeleje, and Liseleje, almost 50 km from Helsingør (*leje* means 'fishing village'). Numerous small chalets, mostly modest hotels, and campsites are the main accommodation in this popular region.

From all round this coast roads lead inland to the delightfully peaceful town of Hillerød, centred on the royal castle of Frederiksborg. The builder-king Christian IV designed and built the present castle, after pulling down the older one where he had been born. The National Historical Museum, administered by the Carlsberg Trust, is housed in the castle. Lovely Grib Skov Wood stretches north for some 10 km from Hillerød, with the lake called Esrum Sø east of it. Another fine royal castle, named Fredensborg (Peace Castle: so called because peace was signed here between Denmark and Sweden in 1620) stands on the lake's further side.

If you continue round Zealand's coast from Liseleje you come by criss-cross roads to the steel-and-explosives town of Frederiksværk, the little herring-fishing town of Nykøbing (Nykøbing Sjælland to distinguish it from its namesakes), the industrial and port town of Holbæk, and ancient Kalundborg, once a major royal stronghold but now known for its manufactures.

Along Zealand's north-west coast ferries operate from Hundested (near Frederiksværk) to Grenaa in Jutland (2½ hours), from Sjællands Odde to Ebeltoft (1½ hours), and from Kalundborg to Samsø island (2 hours), Aarhus (3 hours), and Juelsminde (see Vejle: 2½ hours).

About half way between Nykøbing and Kalundborg, in Faarevejle village church, you can see the Earl of Bothwell, husband of Mary Queen of Scots. Imprisoned for the last 11 years of his life, he was chained to a pillar in the dungeons of Dragsholm Castle, not far from Faarevejle, for the last 5. Mummified by some freak accident his body is still kept in a glass-topped coffin.

Nyborg

Nyborg, on Funen's eastern side and 30 km from Odense, is one end of the Great Belt train-ferry crossing: motorists embarking and disembarking at Knudshoved by-pass it completely. Yet a very pleasant small town lies behind the tangle of railway lines and the busy motorway, with excellent bathing and several hotels, including one of Denmark's best, just north of the town.

Its main point of interest is its castle, of which only one carefully and lovingly restored wing remains out of the original 4.

Scandinavia's oldest royal castle, it was built in 1170 to close the Great Belt to marauding Wendish pirates. From 1282 until 1413 the country's first parliament, called the Danehof, met here. Three wings were destroyed by the Swedes in the war of 1658-60. Today, original geometrical wall-paintings have been uncovered, the royal family has lent furniture going back to the 15th century, and long untended beams and woodwork have been beautifully restored, so that you get a very vivid idea of the castle's appearance in its heyday. Nyborg's church was dedicated by Queen Margrethe in 1388. The Crusaders' House (Korsbrødregaarden) stands close to it. Founded as a monastery in 1396 it was taken over by the Knights Templar in 1441.

Odense

Odense (pronounced roughly like Aw-thencer—though no Dane expects a foreigner to know this) is the capital of Funen island, Denmark's third largest city, an important port as well as industrial centre, and Hans Andersen's birthplace. This last fact bulks so large in most travellers' minds that they hardly ever leave themselves time to discover how pleasant and attractive Odense is.

The city's most staggering modern building is its Town Hall, built in clear rivalry with those of Copenhagen and Aarhus and completed only in 1955. The original one (1880) was unusual enough in having as frontage a facsimile of Siena's ancient Palazzo Pubblico. The new structure retains this façade, while providing a lot of extra accommodation of often revolutionary design and almost unimaginable sumptuousness. Every visible thing except light bulbs and window glass was specially designed. Groups are taken round at fixed hours.

Odense's oldest building, the Cathedral of Sankt Knud (St Canute, not the king we remember but Canute II, 1080-1086), faces the Town Hall across the square. It dates from the 13th century and experts say it is Denmark's finest Gothic church. Like virtually all Danish churches it is brick-built and light and colourful, with a particularly remarkable altarpiece consisting of 300 detachable figures.

St Canute himself—or rather his bones—can be seen in a glass-covered coffin in the crypt. The skull fracture caused by a stone thrown when the mob broke into St Alban's Church in Odense is easily visible. (The old St Alban's disappeared long ago, though there is a modern Albani Kirke.) Canute's shrine was one of two which medieval pilgrims visited. It is possible that the other was occupied by the body of the English monk St Alban. Two 16th-century Danish kings and their queens are also buried in the Cathedral.

Remains of a Benedictine monastery similarly dedicated to St Canute adjoin the Cathedral, with a well kept monastic-style herb garden beside them. Another garden, just beyond the monastery's, is a memorial to Hans Andersen. The River Odense (Odense Aa) flows through it.

No. 3 Munkemøllestræde, where Hans Andersen (always referred to as H.C. Andersen in Danish) lived from the age of 2 till he was 14, is preserved as a museum. It consists of one room and a kitchen. The most important collection of items connected with him is, however, H.C. Andersens Hus (Hans Andersen's House) on the corner of Hans Jensensstraede and Bangs Boder. It incorporates his birthplace. You will find assembled here, apart from copies of his works in 70 or more languages, things which he used, including the rope he always carried in case a hotel where he was staying caught fire, and specimens of his superb cut-out paper designs.

A motor boat trip along the very attractive River Odense, from Munke Mose park to the Zoo and Tivoli amusement gardens (based on Copenhagen's) and on to the Funen Village open-air museum, makes a very pleasant excursion. The Funen Village (Den fynske Landsby) consists of typical old village homes, re-erected in the same way as at Copenhagen's Frilandsmuseum and Aarhus's Den gamle By. A special attraction is the Sortebrokro (Black Bridge Inn), a genuine old village hostelry, with modern kitchens attached which serves excellent food. Other possible excursion places are mentioned under Funen.

Odense has a varied selection of hotels and other accommodation, including a motel on the outskirts suitable for motor tourists, together with numerous restaurants and the collection of late-night spots you expect in any sizeable Danish town.

Randers

Randers is another of the many Danish towns with a long history, a pleasant layout, and numerous modern factories—whose products, in Randers' case, include bacon for a lot of British breakfasts. The 14th-century Sankt Mortens Kirke is perhaps the finest of the town's old buildings. The Town Hall dates from the 18th century, with what is reputedly Randers' oldest surviving building, the Paaskesønnernes Gaard, on its left. A narrow street beside this old house leads to surviving portions of a 15th-century monastery dedicated to the Holy Ghost and now called Helligaandshuset. In the late 18th and early 19th century these housed Randers' 'Latin school' (grammar school), several of whose pupils became famous in Denmark.

Randers lies roughly 40 km east of Viborg and 36 km north of Aarhus.

Rebild National Park and Rold Skov

In 1912 a group of Danish-born American citizens bought a piece of land in the Rebild Hills (Rebild Bakker) about 25 km south of Aalborg and gave it to the Danish Government on condition that a ceremony commemorating the American Declaration of Independence should be held there every July 4th. In 1934 a replica of Lincoln's log cabin was built with materials from each American state and furnished with exhibits illustrating the early pioneers' and Indians' life. Since World War II, in particular, the annual celebration has grown tremendously in importance.

Rold Skov, surrounding the National Park, is extensive enough today, but is only a tiny part of the vast forest which once covered Himmerland, the home—as some scholars think—of the ancient Cimbri tribe. The soil is sandy and dotted with clumps of beeches, though spruce is the commonest tree, and oaks, aspens, heather, rosemary, juniper, whortleberry, and bilberry also grow there. The landscape is decidedly hilly, and cut by deep ravines, with clear lakes in several places. You can enjoy wonderful walks here.

Inside the National Park area a number of buildings have been erected close to the log cabin. They include a restaurant, a Youth Hostel, and the Hjemstavn- og Spillemands Museum devoted to the wandering fiddlers *(spillemænd)* once common in this region, and to their instruments and way of life. A carved stone commemorates also the Cimbri who 'went out from this district 120 BC'.

Apart from the Youth Hostel, accommodation is available at the Rold Stor Kro, a modern hotel beside the A10 main road, in the village of Skørping east of Rold Skov; and in the small town of Hobro, 20 km south on the main road (see also Viking remains).

Ribe

Situated on marshy ground close to the sea in the southern part of the west Jutland coast some 50 km north of Tønder and the German frontier, Ribe is one of Denmark's most interesting towns. Though still small it was first mentioned in history in AD 862 and has been a bishopric since 948—which makes it Denmark's most ancient town. It boasts an outstandingly interesting Cathedral and a lot of old cobbled streets and little timber-frame houses, as well as a castle going back to the 12th century.

The Cathedral, dedicated to Our Lady (Vor Frue), was begun about 1130 and built with stone brought from the Rhineland. Much of the early architecture is Romanesque, but it includes a very unusual (for Europe) Byzantine dome over the nave-transept crossing. The large square tower, intended partly for defence, was first built about 1250 and rebuilt 400 years later. The smaller, south-west tower dates only from 1896, but replaces a medieval structure. Sculpture of almost every date from 1130 to the present decorates the interior, including several works by Anne Marie Carl-Nielsen, the famous composer's wife. The fine organ dates from 1635 and the highly decorative pulpit from 1597.

The fine 15th-century Town Hall stands in the heart of the old town. It was here in 1460 that King Christian I, after becoming Duke of Slesvig (Schleswig in German) and Count of Holstein (Holsten in Danish), issued his famous decree that the two should never be separated—and thus laid the foundation of the 'Schleswig-Holstein question' which bedevilled European politics throughout the 19th century and was only resolved by a plebiscite in 1920 in which North Slesvig opted to be Danish and South Schleswig and Holstein German.

Ribe used to be famous for the storks which came regularly each year to nest on the roofs of old houses. In recent years their numbers have fluctuated, though a few can usually be seen in summer.

Hotels and other accommodation are available in Ribe, including an excellent municipal campsite. The town has a main tourist office.

Ringsted

A capital city in Viking times and a favourite royal centre up to the reign of Christian IV (1588-1648), Ringsted is today a simple market town, notable mainly for its church of St Benedict (Sankt Bendt Kirke). Originally part of a Benedictine monastery founded about 1080, St Benedict's is Denmark's oldest brick-built church and the burial place of many Danish kings and queens of the 13th and 14th centuries. Queen Ingeborg's 14th-century tomb is covered by a brass similar in style to brasses of corresponding date in King's Lynn. Bjernede village, about 12 km west of Ringsted (turn off the A1 at Slaglille), has Zealand's only round church, built like those on Bornholm.

Ringsted lies about 30 km south-west of Roskilde and 60 km from Copenhagen by the A1.

Roskilde

In its early days Roskilde was Denmark's most important city. From 1020 till supplanted by Copenhagen in 1416 it was the seat of the Danish court. Its first church, made of wood, was built by Harald Bluetooth in about 960 and its first bishop, appointed 100 years later, was probably an Englishman. Absalon, founder of Copenhagen, became Bishop of Roskilde in 1157 when he was only 29.

The city's political importance has declined today and it has become instead an important industrial centre. But its Cathedral, reputedly Denmark's finest, still draws tens of thousands of visitors every year. It contains the tombs of all but 3 of Denmark's kings from the last 500 years, and all but 4 of their queens. Margrethe, Queen of Denmark, Norway, and Sweden (died 1412) is also buried here.

The present lofty building, the third since Harald Bluetooth's little wooden church, was started in Romanesque style by Absalon and completed in Gothic a century later. The prominent green spires were added by the indefatigable Christian IV.

You enter through the south porch. Immediately on your right is the earliest of 4 Royal Chapels added to the original groundplan, that of Christian I, built in 1459. A single column supports the vaulted ceiling. The heights of several kings marked on it show a little light-hearted boasting. Christian I claims 7 ft 6 ins (against his real 6 ft 2 ins) and Peter the Great of Russia 6 ft 10 ins. Christian I, Christian III, and Frederik II and their queens are buried here.

Further along on the right steep steps lead to the ornate Frederik V's Chapel, containing the sarcophagi of Christian VI, Frederik V, Christian VII, Frederik VI, Christian VIII, and Frederik VII, who reigned, in that order, from 1730 to 1863.

On the nave's opposite side Christian IV's Chapel is separated from the main church by a lovely ironwork screen, dating from 1618. Christian IV and Frederik III, who between them reigned from 1588 to 1670, lie here. And in the last of the Chapels, added in 1923, are the sarcophagi of Christian IX, Frederik VIII, Christian X, and Frederik IX (1899-1972). Queen Margrethe, Christian V, and Frederik IV are buried behind the high altar.

Apart from its many royal tombs, most of them carved sarcophagi like those of the Danish kings of England in Winchester Cathedral, the church has a fine gilded wood altarpiece (1580), carved choir stalls (1420), a 16th/17th century organ, and an extraordinary 16th-century clock. Mechanical figures strike the hours and quarters; St George's clockwork horse rears up on every hour; and a clockwork dragon just as regularly lets out a piercing squeal. An excellent Viking Ship Museum is the town's other main attraction. Coach tours from many parts of Denmark visit Roskilde.

Rømø island

Separated by 8 km of sea from the low-lying west Jutland coast midway between Ribe and Tønder, Rømø has become a popular holiday area in recent years. It has a magnificently wide sandy beach, backed by extensive dunes, facing the North Sea. The village of Havneby in the south has a modern fishing harbour and there is a museum of local history, the Kommandørgaard, on the island. A causeway links Rømø to the low-lying mainland opposite the little town of Skærbæk.

Samsø island

Samsø, midway between Jutland and north Zealand, has also become popular with holidaymakers in recent years. Apart from a number of good, but slightly pebbly, beaches the island is known for its varied landscapes, picturesque little towns, and numerous old farms. Mainly simple accommodation is available. Ferries operate from Aarhus (2 hours), Hov (east of Horsens in Jutland: $1\frac{1}{4}$ hours), and Kalundborg (2 hours).

Silkeborg, the Silkeborg Lakes, and Skanderborg

This region contains some of the best of Denmark's gentle scenery. It lies about 40 km west of Aarhus and is ideal not only for walking and cycling but also for canoe touring. All necessary gear can be hired from firms in and around Silkeborg at reasonable rates: full information is available from the Silkeborg main tourist office.

The whole region is wooded and intersected with paths, mostly well signposted. Hills surrounding the many lakes include mainland Denmark's highest point, 147 m above sea level, and laughingly named Himmelbjerget (The Sky Mountain). As all the lakes are connected by the River Guden (Guden Aa) and its tributaries, extensive canoe-camping trips are popular. Regular pleasure boat services also operate from Silkeborg to Svejbæk, Himmelbjerget, Laven, and Ry. The most entertaining of the vessels used is the paddle-steamer 'Hjelen', which made its first trip to Himmelbjerget with King Frederik VII on board on June 24th, 1861 and has been in continuous service ever since.

A favourite short walk takes you downhill from Silkeborg's Town Square (Torvet) to the bridge over the Guden and then to the right, along the riverside track to the hotel at Hattenæs. If you continue further you can climb various hills on your left which provide good views. A still longer walk (about 15 km) takes you over the hills to the summit of the Sky Mountain, where there is a hotel and restaurant. There are many other possible trips.

Skanderborg, about 32 km south-east of Silkeborg and on the main A10 highway between Horsens and Aarhus, is another centre from which this region can be explored. In medieval times it was an important royal centre, and its position between two major lakes makes it popular with holidaymakers today.

Silkeborg Museum contains one of the most striking of all Denmark's museum exhibits—the so-called 'Tollund Man'. This is the almost perfectly preserved body of a man, buried in a peat bog about 8 km west of Silkeborg some 2000 years ago and discovered by accident in 1950, rather like the 'Grauballe Man' in Aarhus's Moesgaard Museum (see Aarhus). It is often commented that the Tollund Man has the same facial characteristics as many modern Jutlanders.

Quick visits to the Silkeborg-Skanderborg region can be made by car, excursion coach, or public transport from Aarhus and other centres. Plenty of accommodation of most types is available in the area.

Sønderborg and Als island

Sønderborg is the chief town of Als island, immediately off the extreme southern end of Jutland's east coast. It is connected to the mainland by a bridge across the narrow strait. A ferry runs from Fynshav to Bøjden on Funen ($\frac{3}{4}$ hr). As part of North Slesvig, Sønderborg was concerned in the Prussian wars of 1848-9 and 1864: Dybbøl Mill, where the Danes suffered a disastrous defeat in 1864, lies just across the strait.

In Sønderborg itself the main attractions are the castle, Physical Culture Folk High School, the extensive yacht harbour, and the ancient annual Tilting Festival (Ringrider Fest), held on the 2nd weekend of every July.

The castle stands on a point of land south-west of the town. It contains a delightful chapel, built in 1568-70, that was not only Denmark's first Lutheran church but also the country's first piece of building in Renaissance style. Other rooms are devoted mainly to a military museum of local history. The Folk High School was built in 1952 as Denmark's most modern sports training centre: parties are shown round in summer. The Tilting Festival centres on a competition in which riders aim a lance at a 5 cm ring, as they have been doing for 400 years, and includes processions, football matches, wrestling, and general jollification going on till the early hours.

Sønderborg makes a pleasant base for excursions to places like Dybbøl Mill and the royal manor of Graasten some 13 km beyond it. Als island offers pleasant undulating countryside with attractive small villages and good bathing at such places as Høruphav, 3 km east of Sønderborg; the large Kegnæs peninsula south of Høruphav; Mommark, the old ferry terminal 23 km due east of Sønderborg; and Fynshav, the modern terminal to the north.

Svendborg

Roughly 43 km south of Odense on Funen's southern coast, Svendborg is one of Denmark's busiest and most important yachting centres. It is also a charming small town, with a number of old houses in its centre, and a lovely position overlooking the strait separating it from Taasinge island. As a touring base from which to visit southern Funen, with its hills, woods and numerous manor houses, and the islands of Ærø, Taasinge, and Langeland, it is almost ideal. There is good bathing close to the town and at other points nearby. As Svendborg is a very popular holiday base there is no shortage of accommodation of every type, nor of restaurants and entertainment.

One of the town's special attractions is the Zoological Museum, containing among other things examples of all Denmark's birds. St Nicholas' Church dates from the 13th century. A very pleasant walk leads eastward from the harbour along the shore to the area known as Christiansminde, where there are some hotels. A somewhat antique ship makes excursions to the islands of Taasinge and adjacent Thurø, and a private collection of pipes from all over the world has been turned into a popular museum.

Taasinge and Thurø islands

Connected to Svendborg by a high bridge crossing Svendborg Sound, Taasinge is a very colourful little island. Its main town, Troense, boasts a number of old houses, a school that dates from 1654, and a good little private museum devoted to the days of sailing ships, housed in the old schoolhouse. Valdemar's Castle (originally a 17th-century manor house and now a naval museum) overlooks the sea south of tiny Troense. A large oak close to it is said to be 800 years old. From the top of Bregninge's church tower in the middle of the island you can see half south Funen and the German coast near Flensburg on a clear day. The church itself has a colourful pulpit (1621), gaily decorated pew ends, and several of the model ships normal in all Danish seafaring-area churches. Tiny Thurø, connected to Funen east of Svendborg by a road bridge, offers good bathing as well as places to stay at.

Tønder and surroundings

Once an important port but now several km from the sea, Tønder was founded in the 13th century. Today it is famous for its lace and is a very colourful little town. Several 17th-century houses have survived, including the Town Hall, a 'Latin School' (grammar school), and an old apothecary's shop. The red roof and tall spire of Christ Church (1592, incorporating parts of an older building) are visible for miles across the low-lying flat land surrounding the town, and the church's interior is extraordinarily decorated. The town museum contains a good collection of furniture, ceramics, art, and other items.

Møgeltønder, 5 km west of Tønder on the road to Højer and the sea, is an extremely attractive village of thatched cottages. Løgumkloster, 16 km north, off the A11 road to Ribe, is all that remains of a large Cistercian abbey founded in the 11th or 12th century. The Gothic church, library, sacristy, and vaulted chapter house have survived and can be visited. The marshy countryside round about gives a clear idea of the reclamation work necessary before the land could be made productive.

Vejle and its fjord

Although Vejle is a relatively important manufacturing town it is also, thanks mainly to the lovely, hilly east Jutland fjord on which it stands, one of Denmark's most popular holiday centres. Roughly 30 km north of Kolding on the main A10 the town is hilly enough to be called 'Denmark's Mountain Town'. You can certainly ski there if the snow is thick enough in winter. The town is plentifully supplied with hotels and other accommodation and is famous for the number and quality of its nightspots. It is conveniently close to Jelling and other places of interest.

Vejle's main attraction however is the fjord at whose head it lies. Of all the bays cutting sharply into Jutland's hilly east coast this is undoubtedly the most attractive, combining wooded slopes with a curving shape and pleasant bathing beaches, near all of which you will find good hotels and restaurants.

Vejle's main bathing beach, Albuen, lies on the fjord's north shore. You can bathe also at Tirsbaek, Fakkegrav, and Juelsminde (where the ferries from Kalundborg arrive) on that side of the bay. On the south side Munkebjerg and Hvidbjerg are the best spots. Munkebjerg has a well-known hotel and restaurant on top of its wooded slopes.

Viborg

Viborg is one of Jutland's most ancient and historic towns. Its name comes from the 'Sacred Hill' *(Vi Bjerg)* where pagan gods were once worshipped and where the Cathedral now stands. Kings were elected by chieftains assembled here in ancient times. Here, too, Denmark's first coins were struck during the reign of Canute the Great (1018-1035).

Unfortunately, because of repeated fires, few of the town's buildings go back beyond the 18th century. Viborg was created a bishopric in 1065 and the building of a Cathedral began in 1130 with granite brought all the way from Central Germany. Fires and restoration have left nothing of the old building, but the reconstructed version is still Europe's largest granite church, with towers over 40 m high that are a landmark for miles around. Opposite the Cathedral's west front the Old Town Hall, built in 1728, is now a museum. There are a number of other old houses in Sankt Mogensgade near the Cathedral.

Viborg lies about 80 km south of Aalborg by the A13, and 26 north of Silkeborg. It is a useful base for excursions—to the wooded Dollerup Hills some 8 km south, to Skive on the Limfjord, to Silkeborg, and to the lovely scenery and excellent open-air museum of Hjerl Hede, almost equidistant from Viborg, Skive, and Holstebro. Similar in type to Copenhagen's Frilandsmuseum, Aarhus's Den gamle By, and Odense's Den fynske Landsby, the museum has the advantage of being set in scenery that typifies the sort of countryside from which its houses come. It is also remarkable in being a completely private undertaking.

Viking remains

Apart from the Lindholm Høje graveyard at Nørresundby (see Aalborg) and the Ladby Ship (see Funen), there are important Viking forts at Trelleborg on Zealand (off the A1 about 12-13 km east of Korsør or Halsskov) and at Fyrkat about 4 km south-west of Hobro in Jutland (see Rebild National Park). Though Trelleborg is the more elaborate, both follow the same general plan of an encircling rampart enclosing a number of building groups designed with mathematical precision. Both fortresses can be dated to roughly AD 990, and it is not impossible that they were constructed by Sweyn Forkbeard shortly before his invasion of England.

There are of course numerous Viking relics in Copenhagen's National Museum and in other museums throughout Denmark. But there is one other major outdoor trace of the Vikings worth hunting out. This is the 'Viking Road', known also as the 'Ox Road' because cattle being exported to Germany were driven down it 150 years ago. Running south from Viborg, its first 80 km coincide with the Viborg-Vejle highway, A13. After that it branches off down Jutland's west side. Parts are used today for riding holidays. Local tourist offices will help you find it.

The Faroe Islands

These are parts of Denmark too! The Faroes—the name means 'sheep islands'—are easily accessible, though still remote enough to have retained many medieval customs. They consist of 18 islands which provide superb scenery and excellent walking, trout fishing, and birdwatching. Though roads are good (you can take your own car or hire one) other communications are uncertain because of the weather. Sound accommodation is available. You reach the Faroes by regular air services from Bergen (Norway), Reykjavik (Iceland),

Kobmagergade is one of the new pedestrian streets in Copenhagen

and Copenhagen; or by sea from Esbjerg, Leith (Scotland), or
Copenhagen. English is widely spoken, but prices are not low.
Information for the Faroes is available from the Danish Tourist
Board (address p 23), and direct from· Føroya Ferdamannafelag,
DK-3800 Torshavn.

Language Guide

Pronunciation

Danish is at least as irregular as English: words of apparently similar spellings often are not pronounced alike and letters that are sounded in emphatic or careful speech disappear completely in ordinary conversation. (Unlike most languages, the faster the beginner talks in Danish the easier he will be understood.) Many vowels include glottal stops—as in the Cockney version *li**le bo**le* for 'little bottle'.

Vowels

a	between f*a*t and f*a*ther	
	as in French e	
æ	as in f*a*te	
e	as in f*e*d	—when short
	as in r*a*ther	—at end of word
	as in f*a*te (can replace *æ*)	—when long
i	as in s*i*n	—when short
	as in s*ee*n	—when long
u	as in b*u*ll	—when short
	as in b*oo*t	—when long
y	as French *u* or German *ü*	
ø	as German *ö* (roughly as in f*u*r)	

Diphthongs

aj,ej	as in f*i*re
av,ov	as in h*ow*
ev	as in st*ew*
oj, øj	as in l*oi*ter

Consonants

d	as in *d*og	—at start of word
	silent	—before s,t or after l,n,r
	as in *th*in	—after a vowel
g	as in *g*od at start of word or in *ng*	
	silent	—between two vowels, or finally after vowel
hj	as in *j*ug	
j	as in *y*acht	
v	as in *w*ater	
	as in *v*an	—at start of word or syll.
w	as in *v*an	

Alphabet

The Danish alphabet has 28 letters. Æ, Ø, and Å (in that order) follow Z, and Q is not used. AA is equivalent to Å.

Everyday Expressions

Mr	*Hr*
Mrs	*Fru*
Miss	*Frøken*
Please	*Værs' god*
Thank You	*Tak*
Good Morning	*God morgen*
Good Afternoon	*Goddag*
Good Day	*Goddag*
Good Evening	*God aften*
Good Night	*Godnat*
Good-bye	*Farvel*
Yes	*Ja*
No	*Nej*
How do you do?	*Goddag?*
Very well, and you?	*Goddag?*
Excuse me	*Undskyld*
I am English	*Jeg er engelsk (britisk)*
Do you speak English?	*Taler De engelsk?*
I cannot speak Spanish	*Jeg taler ikke spansk*
I want . . .	*Jeg vil gerne have . . .*
Come in	*Kom ind*
That's all right	*Det er i orden*
You are most kind	*Det er venligt af Dem*
Never mind	*Det gør ikke noget*
Don't worry	*Det skal De ikke bekymre Dem om*
Am I disturbing you?	*Forstyrrer jeg?*
May I introduce . . .	*Må jeg præsentere . . .*
I don't mind	*Jeg har ikke noget imod . . .*
I don't think so	*Det tror jeg ikke*
I am very grateful to you	*Jeg er Dem meget taknemmelig*
What is this (that)?	*Hvad er dette (det)?*
Like this (that)	*Sådan her*
This (that) side	*Denne (den) side*
It is (was) wonderful	*Det er (var) dejligt*
Will this (that) do?	*Kan dette (den) bruges?*
I agree	*Jeg er enig* (I agree with you)
Help yourself	*Tag selv*
What is the time?	*Hvad er klokken?*
In difficulty	
Can you help me?	*Kan De hjælpe mig?*
I am looking for . . .	*Jeg leder efter . . .*
Can you direct me to . . . ?	*Kan De vise mig vej til . . . ?*
I am lost	*Jeg er faret vild*
Where is the British Consulate?	*Hvor er det britiske konsulat?*
Speak slowly	*De bedes tale langsommere*
I am hungry (thirsty)	*Jeg er sulten (tørstig)*
I am busy (tired)	*Jeg har travlt. Jeg er træt*
I am sorry	*Jeg beklager* (I regret). *Undskyld* (Sorry)
What a pity!	*Det var en skam!*
What do you want?	*Hvad ønsker De?*
What do you mean?	*Hvad mener De?*
I do not know	*Det ved jeg ikke*
I do not understand	*Jeg forstår ikke*

I do not agree	*Jeg er ikke enig med Dem*		
I do not like it	*Det kan jeg ikke lide*		
I must go now	*Jeg skal gå nu*		
It is forbidden	*Det er forbudt*		
It is urgent	*Det haster*		
Hurry up!	*Skynd Dem!*		
Be careful	*Vær forsigtig*		
Look out!	*Pas på!*		
Be quiet	*Vær stille* (or: *Ti stille*—stop talking)		

Leave me alone	*Jeg vil gerne være alene*
I shall call a policeman	*Jeg henter en politibetjent*
Help!	*Hjælp!*

after	*efter*	more	*mere*
against	*imod*	much	*meget*
agreed	*enig*	near	*nær*
all	*alle*	next	*næste*
almost	*næsten*	not	*ikke*
among	*mellem*	now	*nu*
before	*før*	on	*på*
behind	*bag*	outside	*udenfor*
below	*under*	over	*over*
beside	*ved siden af*	perhaps	*måske*
between	*mellem*	quick	*hurtig(t)*
cold	*kold*	right	*højre*
downstairs	*nedenunder*	slow	*langsom, langsomt*
elsewhere	*et andet sted*		
enough	*nok*	somebody	*nogen*
everybody	*enhver*	something	*noget*
everything	*alt*	that	*den*
everywhere	*overalt*	there	*der*
except	*undtagen*	these	*disse*
far	*langt*	this	*denne, dette*
for	*for*	those	*de*
here	*her*	through	*gennem*
hot	*varm(t)*	too	*alt for*
in	*i, inde*	towards	*mod*
in front of	*foran*	until	*indtil*
inside	*indeni*	upstairs	*ovenpå*
last	*sidst, sidste*	very	*meget*
left	*venstre*	welcome	*velkomst*
less	*mindre*	when	*når*
listen	*hør*	where	*hvor*
little	*lille, små*	why	*hvorfor*
look	*se, kigge*	without	*uden*
many	*mange*		

Accommodation

I have reserved a room (two rooms)	*Jeg har bestilt et værelse (to værelser)*
I wish to stay for . . .	*Jeg vil gerne blive her i . . .*
I do not want meals	*Uden måltider*
I shall not be here for lunch	*Jeg er ikke her til frokost*
May I take a packed lunch?	*Kan jeg få en madpakke?*
I want breakfast only	*Jeg skal kun have morgenmad*

I want a room with one bed (two beds, a double bed)	*Jeg vil gerne have et værelse med en seng (to senge, en dobbeltseng)*
I want a room with a private bathroom	*Jeg vil gerne have et værelse med bad*
I am on a diet	*Jeg er på diæt*
I cannot eat . . .	*Jeg kan ikke spise . . .*
What are your charges, including (excluding) meals?	*Hvad koster det med (uden) måltider?*
Are there fixed meal times for (breakfast, lunch, dinner)?	*Er der faste spisetider for (morgenmad, frokost, middag)?*
I should like something cheaper	*Jeg vil gerne have noget billigere*
Have you a room with a better view?	*Har De et værelse med en bedre udsigt?*
I want to leave early tomorrow	*Jeg skal rejse tidligt i morgen*
Wake me at . . .	*Jeg vil gerne vækkes klokken . . .*
Can I have my clothes pressed?	*Kan jeg få noget tøj presset?*
Can I have my shoes cleaned?	*Kan jeg få mine sko børstet?*
Can I drink the water from the tap?	*Er der drikkevand i denne hane?*
I want a hot bath	*Jeg vil gerne have et varmt bad*
Is there a plug for my electric razor?	*Er der el-stik til shaver?*
What is the voltage?	*Hvad er el-spændingen?*
I have some things to be washed	*Jeg har noget, der skal vaskes*
Will you get this mended?	*Jeg vil gerne have dette repareret?*
When will they be ready?	*Hvornår vil det være færdigt?*
When does the hotel close?	*Hvornår lukker hotellet?*
I shall be very late	*Jeg kommer sent hjem*
May I have a key?	*Må jeg få en nøgle?*
Is there a night porter?	*Er der en natportier?*
Forward my mail to this address	*Vil De videresende post til denne adresse*

armchair	*lænestol*	coat-hanger	*bøjle*
bath	*bad*	cook	*kok*
bathroom	*badeværelse*	curtain	*gardin*
bed	*seng*	dining-room	*spisestue, restaurant*
bedroom	*soveværelse*		
bedroom (single, double)	*værelse (enkelt, dobbelt)*	eiderdown	*dyne*
(with twin beds)	*(med to senge)*	floor (storey)	*etage*
		hotel	*hotel*
(with a double bed)	*(med en dobbeltseng)*	hotel-keeper	*hotelejer*
		hot-water bottle	*varmedunk*
bell	*klokke*	key	*nøgle*
better	*bedre*	large	*stor, stort*
bill	*regning*	larger	*større*
blanket	*tæppe*	lavatory	*toilet, wc*
blind	*blind*	lift	*elevator*
boarding-house	*pension*	manager	*direktør*
board (full)	*fuld pension*	mattress	*madrasse*
board (half)	*halvpension*	office	*kontor*
bolster	*skråpude*	pillow	*pude*
bulb (electric light)	*pære*	plug (electric)	*stikprop*
		porter	*hotelkarl*
chair	*stol*	proprietor	*ejer*
chambermaid	*stuepige*	quiet	*rolig, roligt*
		quieter	*roligere*

radiator	*radiator*
reading-lamp	*læselampe*
sheet	*lagen*
shower	*brusebad*
shutter	*skodde*
sitting-room	*opholdsstue*
small	*lille*
smaller	*mindre*
soap	*sæbe*

staircase	*trappe*
switch (light)	*kontakt (lys)*
table	*bord*
terrace	*terrasse*
towel	*håndklæde*
wardrobe	*klædeskab*
washbasin	*håndvask*
window	*vindue*

Beach and Bathing

Where is the beach?	*Hvor er badestranden?*
Where can I bathe?	*Hvor kan man bade?*
Is it safe to swim here?	*Er det sikkert at bade her?*
Is it deep or shallow?	*Er der dybt eller lavt vand?*
Is the beach sandy or pebbly?	*Er stranden med sand eller sten?*
I want to hire a . . .	*Jeg vil gerne leje en . . .*
Where can I change?	*Hvor kan man klæde sig om?*
I cannot swim very well	*Jeg er ikke en god svømmer*
Help! Someone is drowning!	*Hjælp! Der er nogen der drukner!*
Can I go underwater swimming here?	*Er der undervandssvømning her?*
Bathing prohibited	*Badning forbudt*

air mattress	*luftmadras*
bathe, to	*at gå i vandet, svømme*
bathing cap	*badehætte*
bathing costume	*badedragt*
bathing hut	*badehus*
beach	*strand*
boat	*båd*
buoy	*bøje*
canoe	*kano*
cliff	*klint, skræt, brink*
coast	*kyst*
crab	*krabbe*
current	*strøm*
danger	*fare*
deckchair	*liggestol*
dive, to	*dykke, dukke, at*
fish, to	*at fiske*
fish	*fisk*
flippers	*svømmefod*
harpoon	*harpun*
jellyfish	*vandmand, vandmænd*

knife	*kniv*
lifebelt	*redningsbælte*
lighthouse	*fyrtårn*
mask	*maske, dække*
octopus	*blæksprutte*
pebble	*sten*
raft	*tømmerflåde, flåde*
rock	*klippe*
rowing boat	*robåd*
sand	*sand*
sea	*hav*
shark	*haj*
shell	*muslingeskal, konkylie*
snorkel	*schnorkel*
speargun	*spydkanon*
sun	*sol*
sunshade	*solskærm*
surf board	*planke til surfriding*
beach umbrella	*strandparasol*
tide	*tidevand*
towel	*håndklæde*

Camping

Where does this road lead?	*Hvor går denne vej hen?*
How far is it to . . .?	*Hvor langt er der til . . . ?*
What is the name of this place?	*Hvad hedder stedet her?*
Is there a Youth Hostel near here?	*Er der et vandrerhjem i nærheden?*
Can we cut across country?	*Kan man skyde genvej?*
We are lost	*Vi er faret vild*

We are looking for a camping site | Vi prøver at finde en campingplads
May we light a fire? | Må der tændes bål?
Where is the toilet (washroom)? | Hvor er toilettet (vaskerummet)
I should like to hire a bicycle | Jeg vil gerne leje en cykel
Where can I buy methylated spirit (paraffin)? | Hvor kan man købe denatureret sprit (petroleum)?

bottle opener	*flaskeåbner*	path	*sti*
bucket	*spand*	penknife	*lommekniv*
camp	*teltlejr*	river	*å, flod*
camping	*camping*	road	*vej*
equipment	*udstyr*	rope	*reb*
camping site	*campingplads*	rubbish	*affald*
candle	*stearinlys*	sandwich	*stykke*
caravan	*campingvogn*		*smørrebrød*
country	*land*	saucepan	*gryde*
field	*mark*	sleeping-bag	*sovepose*
ground-sheet	*teltunderlag*	store	*butik*
haversack	*skråtaske*	tent	*telt*
hitch-hike	*rejse på tommelfinger*	tent peg	*teltpløk*
		thermos	*termoflaske*
hill	*bakke*	tin opener	*dåseåbner*
inn	*kro*	torch (electric)	*lommelygte*
lake	*sø*	waterproof	*vandtæt*
matches	*tændstikker*	wood	*træ*
mountain	*bjerg*		

Church

Where is a Roman Catholic church (Protestant church, synagogue, mosque)? | Hvor er der en katolsk kirke (protestantisk kirke, synagoge, moske)?
At what time are the services held? | Hvornår er der gudstjeneste?

Colours

black	*sort*	orange	*orange*
blue	*blå(t)*	pink	*lyserød(t)*
brown	*brun(t)*	purple	*purpur,*
cream	*flødefarvet*		*blåligrød(t)*
crimson	*højrød(t)*	red	*rød(t)*
fawn	*lysebrun(t)*	scarlet	*purpurrød(t)*
gold	*gylden(t)*	silver	*sølvgrå(t)*
green	*grøn(t)*	violet	*violet*
grey	*grå(t)*	white	*hvid(t)*
mauve	*grålilla, lysviolet*	yellow	*gul(t)*

Days of the Week

Sunday	*søndag*	Thursday	*torsdag*
Monday	*mandag*	Friday	*fredag*
Tuesday	*tirsdag*	Saturday	*lørdag*
Wednesday	*onsdag*		

Months

January	*januar*	July	*juli*
February	*februar*	August	*august*
March	*marts*	September	*september*
April	*april*	October	*oktober*
May	*maj*	November	*november*
June	*juni*	December	*december*

Entertainment

Where is a good cheap night club? — *Hvor er der en god, billig natrestaurant?*
Would you care to dance? — *Må jeg danse med Dem?*
Where can I dance? — *Hvor kan man danse?*
What would you like to drink? — *Hvad ønsker De at drikke?*

band	*orkester*	night club	*natklub*
box	*kasse*	seat	*plads*
box office	*billetkontor*	stage	*scene*
casino	*spillekasino*	stall	*orkesterplads*
cinema	*biograf*	theatre	*teater*
interval	*pause*		

Food and Restaurants

Where is a good (cheap) restaurant? — *Hvor er der en god (billig) restaurant?*
Where is a quick-service restaurant? — *Hvor er der et cafeteria?*
Where is a good restaurant for sea-food? — *Hvor er der en god fiske-restaurant?*
Where is a good restaurant for local dishes? — *Hvor er der en restaurant med lokale specialiteter?*
Can we lunch here? — *Må vi få noget frokost?*
I should like a table near the window — *Jeg vil gerne have et bord ved vinduet*
I only want a snack — *Jeg skal bare have en hurtig ret*
I am in a hurry — *Jeg skal skynde mig*
I should like to wash my hands — *Jeg vil gerne vaske hænder*
Have you the menu? — *Har De et spisekort?*
I like it underdone (medium) (well done) — *Understegt (mellemstegt) (godt stegt)*
A little more — *Lidt mere*
That's too much — *Det er for meget*
I did not order this — *Det har jeg ikke bestilt*
Bring me another — *Må jeg få en andere*
This is cold — *Det er koldt*
I have had enough — *Jeg er mæt*
May I have the bill? — *Må jeg bede om regningen?*
Is the service included? — *Er betjening inkluderet?*
Is this correct? — *Er det rigtigt?*
Please check it — *Vil De regne efter*
I made a mistake — *Det var min fejl*
I'm sorry — *Undskyld*
Keep the change — *Behold byttepengene*
We enjoyed the meal — *Vi nød maden*

ashtray	*askebæger*	bill	*regning*
bar	*bar*	bottle	*flaske*

canned	*på dåse*	plate	*tallerken*
clean	*ren(t)*	saucer	*underkop*
cork	*prop, kork*	serviette, napkin	*serviet*
cup	*kop*	spoon	*ske*
dirty	*snavset*	tablecloth	*dug*
fork	*gaffel*	teapot	*tekande*
fresh	*frisk*	tip	*drikkepenge*
glass	*glas*	waiter	*tjener*
not fresh	*ikke frisk*	waiter (head)	*overtjener*
knife	*kniv*	waiter (wine)	*vintjener*
meal	*måltid, ret*	waitress	*servitrice*
menu, bill of fare	*spisekort*	water-jug	*vandkande*
not clean	*ikke ren*	wine list	*vinkort*

Food   **mad, fødevarer**

apple	*æble*	kidney	*nyre*
apricot	*abrikos*	lamb	*lam*
artichoke	*artiskok*	lemon	*citron*
asparagus	*asparges*	lettuce	*grøn salat*
bacon	*bacon*	liver	*lever*
banana	*banan*	lobster	*hummer*
beans	*bønner*	marmalade	*orangemarmalade*
beef	*oksekød*	melon	*melon*
biscuit	*kiks*	mushroom	*champignon*
bread (white)	*franskbrød*	mussels	*muslinger*
bread (brown)	*sigtebrød*	mustard	*sennep*
butter	*smør*	oil	*olie*
cabbage	*kål*	olive oil	*olivenolie*
cake	*kage*	onion	*løg*
carrot	*gulerod*	orange	*applesin*
cauliflower	*blomkål*	oyster	*østers*
caviare	*kaviar*	pastry (cake)	*wienerbrød*
celery	*selleri*	peach	*fersken*
cheese	*ost*	peanuts	*jordnødder*
cherries	*kirsebær*	pear	*pære*
chicken	*kylling*	peas	*ærter*
chocolate	*chokolade*	pepper	*peber*
chops	*koteletter*	pickles	*pickles*
crab	*krabbe*	pineapple	*ananas*
crayfish	*krebs*	plum	*blomme*
cream	*fløde*	pork	*flæskekød*
cucumber	*agurk*	potato	*kartoffel*
dessert	*dessert*	prawn	*stor reje*
egg	*æg*	prunes	*svesker*
figs	*figner*	raisins	*rosiner*
fish	*fisk*	raspberry	*hindbær*
fruit	*frugt*	rice	*ris*
game	*vildt*	roll	*rundstykke*
garlic	*hvidløg*	salad	*salat*
grapefruit	*grapefrugt*	salmon	*laks*
ham	*skinke*	salt	*salt*
honey	*honning*	sardine	*sardin*
hors-d'oeuvres	*forret*	sauce	*sovs*
ice	*is*	sausage (beef)	*pølse*
ice-cream	*is*	sausage (pork)	*pølse*
jam	*syltetøj*	scampi	*scampi*

seafood	*fiskemad*	sugar	*sukker*
shrimp	*reje*	toast	*ristet brød*
snail	*snegl*	tomato	*tomat*
sole	*søtunge*	trout	*ørred*
soup	*suppe*	vanilla	*vanilje*
spinach	*spinat*	veal	*kalvekød*
steak	*bøfkød*	vegetables	*grøntsager*
strawberry	*jordbær*	vinegar	*eddike*

Drink

What would you like to drink?		*Hvad ønsker De at drikke?*
What would you suggest?		*Hvad vil De foreslå?*
I should like . . .		*Jeg vil gerne have . . .*
Your health!		*Skål!*
Just a little		*Kun lidt*
A little more		*Lidt mere*
That's enough		*Tak, det er nok*

alcoholic drink	*spiritus*	mineral water	*mineralvand*
another	*en til*	mug	*krus*
aperitif	*aperitif*	nip	*en lille*
beer	*øl*	orange	*appelsin*
bottle (half)	*flaske (halv)*	orangeade	*orangeade*
brandy	*cognac*	port	*portvin*
carafe	*karaffel*	rum	*rom*
champagne	*champagne*	sherry	*sherry*
cider	*æblevin*	small	*lille*
cocktail	*cocktail*	soda water	*soda*
double	*dobbelt*	spirits	*spiritus*
gin	*gin*	tonic water	*tonic*
glass	*glas*	vermouth	*vermouth*
ice	*is*	vodka	*vodka*
jug	*kande*	water	*vand*
lager	*pilsner*	whisky	*whisky*
large	*stor*	wine, dry	*vin, tør*
lemon	*citron*	wine, sweet	*vin, sød*
lemonade	*lemonade*	wine, red	*rødvin*
lime	*lime*	wine, rosé	*rose-vin*
chocolate	*chokolade*	wine, white	*hvidvin*
coffee (white)	*kaffe (med fløde)*	wine, local	
coffee (black)	*kaffe*	milk-shake	*milk-shake*
milk	*mælk*	tea (lemon)	*te (med citron)*
liqueur	*likør*	tea (milk)	*te (med mælk)*
non-alcoholic	*alkoholfri*		

Health

Send for a doctor	*Send bud efter lægen*
It is broken	*Er den (det) brækket*
Have you any bandages?	*Har De forbindingssager?*
Do not move him (her)	*Han (hun) må ikke flyttes*
I am not feeling well	*Jeg har det skidt*
I have a pain here	*Det gør ondt her*
I have a headache	*Jeg har hovedpine*
I have a sore throat	*Jeg er øm i halsen*
My stomach is upset	*Der er noget i vejen med maven*
I feel much better	*Jeg har det meget bedre*

English	Danish	English	Danish
Can you recommend a dentist?	*Kan De anbefale en tandlæge?*		
I have a toothache	*Jeg har tandpine*		
I want it out	*Den skal trækkes ud*		
I should like an injection	*Jeg vil gerne have en indsprøjtning*		
You are hurting me	*Det gør ondt*		
Can you make up this prescription?	*Må jeg få en recept?*		
When will it be ready?	*Hvornår er det færdigt?*		
Can you give me a remedy for . . . ?	*Kan De give mig noget for . . . ?*		
For external use only	*Kun til udvortes brug*		
One teaspoonful (tablespoonful) in a glass of water	*En teskefuld (spiseskefuld) i et glas vand*		

accident	*ulykke*	hospital	*sygehus*
ambulance	*ambulance*	illness	*sygdom*
bandage	*bandage*	indigestion	*mavebesvær*
bite	*bid*	injection	*indsprøjtning*
bleeding	*bløder*	insomnia	*søvnløshed*
blister	*vabel*	nausea	*kvalme*
boil	*byld*	nurse	*sygeplejerske*
burn (scald)	*skolde*	pain	*ondt*
cold	*kold(t)*	poison	*gift*
constipation	*konstipation*	remedy	*lægemiddel*
cough	*hoste*	sick, to feel	*at have kvalme*
cramp	*krampe*	sore throat	*øm hals*
cut	*sår*	sprain	*forstuvning*
dangerous	*farlig(t)*	sting	*stik*
dentist	*tandlæge*	stomach-ache	*mavepine*
diarrhoea	*diarré*	sunburn	*solbrændthed*
diet	*diæt*	sunstroke	*solstik*
doctor	*doktor*	surgery	*konsultations-værelse*
faint	*besvimelse*		
fever	*feber*	swelling	*bullenskab*
filling (stopping)	*plombe*	temperature	*temperatur*
gas	*gas*	toothache	*tandpine*
hay-fever	*høfeber*	vomit	*opkast*
headache	*hovedpine*	wound	*sår*
Chemist	**Apoteker**		
aspirin	*aspirin*	prescription	*recept*
cotton wool	*vat*	quinine	*kinin*
gargle	*gurglemiddel*	sanitary towel	*hygiejnebind*
gauze	*gaze*	sleeping-pill	*sovepille*
iodine	*jod*	smelling-salts	*lugtesalt*
laxative	*afføringsmiddel*	sticking-plaster	*hæfteplaster*
medicine	*medicin*	toilet paper	*toiletpapir*
powder (talcum)	*pudder (talkum)*	vaseline	*vaseline*

Money/Banks

Where is the nearest bank?	*Hvor er den nærmeste bank?*
May I see the manager?	*Må jeg tale med direktoren?*
Will you cash this (traveller's) cheque?	*Jeg vil gerne veksle denne (rejse) check?*
What is the exchange rate for the pound sterling?	*Hvad er kursen på pund?*
How much is this worth?	*Hvad får jeg for dette?*
I should like some small change	*Jeg vil gerne have nogle småpenge*

bank	*bank*
cash, to	*veksle*
change	*byttepenge*
cheque	*check*
coin	*mønt*
exchange (rate)	*vekselkurs*
letter of credit	*rejseakkreditiv*
money	*penge*

money exchange bureau	*vekselkontor*
note	*pengeseddel*
pound sterling	*pund sterling*
rate	*kurs*
traveller's cheque	*rejsecheck*

Motoring

Do you know the road to . . . ? *Kan De vise mig vej til . . . ?*
How far is it to . . . ? *Hvor langt er der til . . .?*
I want some petrol (oil, water) *Jeg vil gerne have benzin (olie, vand)*
I need . . . litres *Jeg vil gerne have . . . liter* (you
mostly buy by amount of money)
Have you distilled water for my battery? *Har De destilleret vand til batteriet?*

Check the tyre pressures *Vil De kontrollere dæktrykkene*
The pressure should be . . . in front and . . . at the back *. . . i forhjulene og . . . i baghjulene*
I have had a breakdown (puncture) *Jeg har motorstop (jeg er punkteret)*

Where can I find a mechanic? *Hvor kan jeg få fat i en mekaniker?*
Do you do repairs? *Kan De påtage Dem reparationen?*
I have broken . . . *Min . . . er knækket*
This does not work *Den (det) virker ikke*
Can you do it immediately? *Kan det ordnes med det samme?*
How long must I wait? *Hvor længe varer det?*
Where can I park? *Hvor må jeg parkere?*
I want to hire a car *Jeg vil gerne leje en vogn*
How much an hour (a day)? *Hvor meget koster det i timen (per dag)?*

Is there an English-speaking driver? *Er der en engelsktalende fører?*

Go more quickly *Kør hurtigere*
Do not drive so fast *De kører for hurtigt*
Wait here (over there) *Vent her (derovre)*
Pick me up at . . . *Jeg vil gerne hentes klokken . . .*
I must be back by . . . *Jeg skal være tilbage klokken . . .*

back axle	*bagaksel*
boot	*bagagerum*
brake	*bremse*
breakdown	*motorstop*
breakdown truck	*kranvogn*
can	*dåse, dunk*
car	*bil, vogn*
caravan	*campingvogn*
clutch	*kobling*
convertible	*cabriolet*
cross-roads	*vejkryds*
danger	*fare*
distilled water	*destilleret vand*
drive, to	*køre, til*
driver	*fører*
driving licence	*kørekort*

exhaust	*udblæsning*
garage	*garage*
gear box	*gearkasse*
gear lever	*gearstang*
ignition key	*tændingsnøgle*
jack	*donkraft*
lever	*arm*
lights	*lygter*
lubrication	*smøring*
mechanic	*mekaniker*
motorway	*motorvej*
narrow road	*smal vej*
no entry	*indkørsel forbudt*
no parking	*parkering forbudt*
oil	*olie*
overtaking prohibited	*overhaling forbudt*

parking	*parkering*
pedestrian	*fodgænger*
pedestrian crossing	*fodgænger-overgang*
petrol	*benzin*
petrol pump	*benzinepumpe*
radiator	*køler*
repairs	*reparationer*
reverse	*bak*
road block	*vejspærring*
road junction	*vejknudepunkt*
roadworks	*vejarbejde*
roundabout	*rundkørsel*
school	*skole*
screw	*skrue*
screwdriver	*skruetrækker*
skid	*skride ud*

slippery surface	*glat vejbane*
slow down	*kør langsomt*
spanner	*skruenøgle*
speed	*hastighed*
speed limit	*hastighed-sbegrænsning*
steep hill	*stejl bakke*
steering wheel ·	*rat*
tank	*tank*
traffic lights	*trafiklys*
tyre	*dæk*
tyre (tubeless)	*dæk (slangeløst)*
two-stroke mixture	*totaktsblanding*
uneven road	*ujævn vej*
unscrew, to	*skrue ud, at*
wheel	*hjul*

Numbers

1	*en*		18	*atten*
2	*to*		19	*nitten*
3	*tre*		20	*tyve*
4	*fire*		21	*en-og-tyve*
5	*fem*		22	*to-og-tyve*
6	*seks*		30	*tredive*
7	*syv*		31	*en-og-tredive*
8	*otte*		32	*to-og-tredive*
9	*ni*		40	*fyrre*
10	*ti*		41	*en-og-fyrre*
11	*elleve*		50	*halvtreds*
12	*tolv*		60	*tres*
13	*tretten*		70	*halvfjerds*
14	*fjorten*		80	*firs*
15	*femten*		90	*halvfems*
16	*seksten*		100	*hundrede*
17	*sytten*			

Photography

I want a black and white (colour) film for this camera

Jeg vil gerne have en sort/hvid (farve) film til dette fotografiapparat

Have you any fast film? *Har De en hurtig film?*
Will you load my camera? *Vil De sætte den i apparatet?*
Will you develop and print this film? *Kan De fremkalde denne film og lave aftryk?*
I want one (two, three, etc) print(s) of each *Jeg vil gerne have et (to, tre, osv) aftryk af hvert*
When will they be ready? *Hvornår er de færdige?*
I must have them by . . . *Jeg skulle gerne have Dem inden . . .*

camera	*kamera*
ciné camera	*filmkamera*
colour	*farve*
develop, to	*fremkalde, at*
enlargement	*forstørrelse*
exposure meter	*belysningsmåler*
film	*film*
film winder	*filmspole*
filter	*filter*
lens	*linse*
lens-hood	*modlysblænder*
negative	*negativ*
print	*aftryk*
range-finder	*afstandsmåler*
shutter	*lukker*
view-finder	*søger*

Post Office

Where is the nearest post office?	*Hvor er det nærmeste postkontor?*
Can I have a stamp for this letter?	*Må jeg bede om et frimærke til · dette brev?*
I want to express this letter	*Jeg vil gerne have dette brev sendt som ekspres*
I want to register this letter	*Jeg vil gerne have dette brev sendt anbefalet*
I want to send this parcel	*Jeg vil gerne sende denne pakke*
Have you any letters poste restante for me?	*Er der poste restante breve til mig?*
I want to send a telegram to . . .	*Jeg vil gerne sende et telegram til . . .*
What is the charge per word?	*Hvad koster det per ord?*
I want a telephone call to England	*Jeg vil gerne ringe til England*
Will you get me this number?	*Kan De skaffe mig dette nummer?*
How much will it be?	*Hvad vil det koste?*
You gave me the wrong number	*Jeg fik forkert nummer*

call (telephone)	*telefonsamtale*	post office	*postkontor*
collection (of post)	*tømning*	postal order	*postanvisning*
		postman	*postbud*
directory	*telefonbog*	number	*nummer*
international money order	*international postanvisning*	register, to	*anbefalet*
		reply	*svar*
letter	*brev*	paid	*betalt*
letter-box	*postkasse*	stamp	*frimærke*
parcel	*pakke*	telegram	*telegram*
postcard	*postkort*	telephone	*telefon*

Public Notices

close, to	*lukke*	open	*åben*
cross now	*gå*	pull	*træk*
engaged	*optaget*	push	*tryk*
gentlemen	*herrer*	ring (the bell)	*ring*
information	*information*	stop, to	*standse, at*
knock	*banke*	toilet	*toilet*
ladies	*damer, kvinder*	vacant	*fri*
no entry	*adgang forbudt*	wait	*vente*
no smoking	*tobaksrygning forbudt*	way in	*indgang*
		way out	*udgang*
occupied	*optaget*		

Shopping

Where can I find a . . . ?	*Hvor kan jeg finde en (et) . . . ?*
How much is . . . ?	*Hvad koster . . . ?*
I want to buy . . .	*Jeg vil gerne købe . . .*
Have you anything cheaper?	*Har De noget billigere?*
I want more (less) than that	*Jeg skal have mere (mindre) end det*
I will buy this	*Jatak*
That's all	*Det er det hele*
It doesn't fit me	*Den (det) passer mig ikke*
It doesn't work	*Den (det) virker ikke*
Can you change it?	*Kan den (det) byttes?*
Will you change it later?	*Kan den (det) byttes senere?*
Can you refund my money?	*Kan man få pengene tilbage?*
My English size is . . .	*På engelsk er min størrelse . . .*

Will you measure me?	*Kan De måle mig?*
May I try this on?	*Må jeg prøve denne her?*
Can I order one (some)?	*Kan jeg bestille en (nogle)?*
Send it to this address	*Kan De sende den (det) til denne adresse?*
I will return later	*Jeg kommer igen senere*
It is too large (small)	*Den (det) er for stor (lille)*
How much each (per kilo, etc.)?	*Hvor meget koster den (det) per styk (per kilo)?*
Are these ripe (fresh)?	*Er de modne (friske)?*

Repairs

I have broken (torn) this	*Den (det) her er gået i stykker*
Can you repair it?	*Kan De reparere den (det)?*
When will it be ready?	*Hvornår er den (det) færdig?*
I have to leave by . . .	*Jeg skal rejse den . . .*

Hairdressing

I want a haircut	*Jeg vil gerne klippes*
I want my hair trimmed	*Jeg skal blot studses*
Don't cut it too short	*Ikke for kort*
I don't want any oil on my hair	*Ingen brilliantine i håret*
I want a shave	*Jeg vil gerne barberes*
Trim my moustache (beard)	*Mit overskæg (skæg) skal studses*
I want this style (show design)	*Som dette her*
I want a shampoo and set	*Jeg vil gerne have håret vasket og friseret*
I want a permanent wave	*Jeg vil gerne permanentkrølles*
I want a bleach (colour rinse) (tint)	*Jeg skal have håret bleget (farvet)*
I want a manicure (pedicure)	*Jeg vil gerne have manicure (pedicure)*
I want a face massage	*Jeg vil gerne have ansigtsmassage*
Thank You. That's very nice	*Tak, det er fint*
Could I make an appointment for . . . o'clock?	*Kan jeg få en aftale til klokken . . .?*

antiques	*antikviteter*	cheap	*billig*
bag	*pose*	cheaper	*billigere*
baker	*bager*	chemist	*apotek*
ballpoint	*kuglepen*	chiropodist	*fodplejer*
bathing suit	*badedragt*	cigar	*cigar*
bath salts	*badesalt*	cigarette lighter	*cigartænder*
battery	*batteri*	cleaner	*renseri*
belt	*bælte, rem*	clock	*ur*
better	*bedre*	clothes	*tøj*
blouse	*bluse*	coat	*frakke*
book	*bog*	coffee	*kaffe*
bookseller	*boghandler*	collar	*krave*
bracelet	*armbånd*	comb	*kam*
braces	*seler*	colour rinse	*toning*
brassiere	*brystholder, bh*	cotton	*bomuld*
brooch	*broche*	cosmetics	*kosmetik*
brush	*børste*	cushion	*pude*
butcher	*slagter*	cuff-links	*manchetknapper*
button	*knap*	cup	*kop*
camera	*kamera*	dark	*mørk*
cardigan	*cardigan*	darker	*mørkere*

delicatessen	charcuteri
department store	stormagasin
dictionary	ordbog
disinfectant	desinficerings-middel
doll	dukke
draper	manufaktur-handler
dress	kjole
drycleaner	kemisk renseri
ear-rings	øreringe
elastic	elastik
envelope	konvolut
expensive	dyr(t)
fancy leather goods	kunstlæder
face powder	pudder
fine	fin(t)
finer	finere
fishmonger	fiskehandler
florist	blomsterhandler
fork	gaffel
fur	pels
glasses	glas
gloves	handsker
gold	guld
gramophone record	grammofonplade
greengrocer	grønthandler
grocer	købmand
guide book	turistfører
handbag	håndtaske
hat	hat
heavy	tung(t)
heavier	tungere
heel	hæl
high	høj(t)
ink	blæk
invisible mending	kunststopning
ironmonger	isenkræmmer
jacket	jakke
jeweller	juvelér
label	mærke
large	stor(t)
larger	større
laundry	vaskeri
leather	læder
light(er) (weight)	let(tere)
light(er) (colour)	lys(ere)
lighter flint	flintsten
lipstick	læbestift
long	lang(t)
longer	længere
loose	løs(t)
looser	løsere
low	lav(t)
magazine	blad
manicure	manicure
map	kort
matches	tændstikker
material	stof
nail	negl
nail-brush	neglebørste
nail-file	neglefil
narrow	smal(t)
narrower	smallere
necklace	halsbånd
needle	nål
newsagent	aviskiosk
newspaper	avis
nightdress	natkjole
nylons	nylonstrømper
pale	bleg
pants (men's)	underbukser
panties	dametrusser
pen	pen
pencil	blyant
perfume	parfume
photographer	fotograf
pin (safety)	sikkerhedsnål
pipe	pipe
plate	tallerken
powder	pudder
powder compact	pudderdåse
powder puff	pudderkvast
purse	pung
pyjamas	pyjamas
radio	radio
raincoat	regnfrakke
razor	barbermaskine
razor blade	barberblad
refill	refill
ribbon	bånd
rollers (hair)	curlers
sandals (rope-soled)	sandaler (med rebsåler)
saucer	underkop
scarf	halstørklæde
scissors	saks
shampoo	shampoo
shaving cream	barbercreme
shaving soap	barbersæbe
shawl	sjal
shirt	skjorte
shoes	sko
shoe-laces	snorebånd
shop	butik
shop assistant	ekspedient

short	*kort(t)*	sweater	*sweater*
shorter	*kortere*	sweets	*bolcher*
shorts	*shorts*	tailor	*skrædder*
silk	*silke*	tea	*te*
silver	*sølv*	tie	*slips*
size	*størrelse*	tin	*dåse*
skirt	*nederdel*	thick	*tyk(t)*
slip	*underkjole*	thicker	*tykkere*
slippers	*slippers*	thin	*tynd(t)*
small	*lille*	thread	*tråd*
smaller	*mindre*	tight	*stram(t)*
soap	*sæbe*	tighter	*strammere*
socks	*sokker*	tobacco	*tobak*
spectacles	*briller*	tobacconist	*tobakshandler*
spoon	*ske*	toothbrush	*tandbørste*
stationer	*papirhandler*	toothpaste	*tandpasta*
stockings	*strømper*	toy	*legetøj*
strap (watch)	*rem*	trousers	*bukser*
string	*snor*	umbrella	*paraply*
strong	*stærk(t)*	underwear	*undertøj*
stronger	*stærkere*	vacuum flask	*termoflaske*
suede	*ruskind*	wallet	*tegnebog*
suit	*sæt tøj*	watch	*ur*
suitcase	*kuffert*	wide	*bred(t)*
sun-lotion	*sol-lotion*	wider	*bredere*
sun-glasses	*solbriller*	wine	*vin*
suntan cream (oil)	*sol-creme (-olie)*	writing paper	*skrivebord*
		zip	*lynlås*

Sightseeing

What is there of interest to see?	*Havd er der at se af interesse?*
Is there a tourist information bureau here?	*Er der et turistkontor her?*
Is there an English-speaking guide?	*Er der en engelsktalende guide?*
I don't want a guide	*Jeg ønsker ingen guide*
I want to go to . . .	*Jeg vil gerne til . . .*
How much is this excursion?	*Hvad koster denne rundtur?*
Are there any boat trips?	*Er der ture med båd?*
How long does it take?	*Hvor længe varer det (den)?*
What time does the trip begin?	*Hvad tid begynder turen?*
When do I get back?	*Hvornår kommer man tilbage?*
We want to be together	*Vi vil gerne være sammen*
Can I go in?	*Må jeg gå indenfor?*
Is this the way to . . . ?	*Er dette vejen til . . . ?*
How far is it from here to . . . ?	*Hvor langt er der herfra til . . . ?*
How long will it take?	*Hvor længe varer det?*
I want a quick look round the town	*Jeg vil gerne have en hurtig tur rundt i byen*
Which way?	*Hvad vej?*
This (that) way	*Denne (den) vej*
I am lost	*Jeg er faret vild*

archaeology	*arkæologi*	cable-car	*kabine i tovbane*
battlement	*brystværn*	castle	*slot*
bridge	*bro*	cathedral	*domkirke*
building	*bygning*	church	*kirke*

city	*by*	monument	*monument*
coast	*kyst*	mountain	*bjerg*
excursion	*udflugt*	mountain	*bjergbane*
fountain	*springvand*	railway	
gallery (art)	*kunstgalleri*	pottery	*lertøj*
gallery	*kunstmuseum*	(product)	
(museum)		rest, to	*hvile, at*
garden	*have*	river	*flod*
gate	*port, indgang*	ruins	*ruiner*
gorge	*slugt, kløft*	seat	*plads*
guide	*fører*	square	*plads*
gulf	*havbugt* (if sea)	street	*gade*
interpreter	*tolk*	town hall	*rådhus*
lake	*sø*	valley	*dal*
law courts	*domhuset*	village	*landsby*
lighthouse	*fyrtårn*		

Sport

Do you play . . . ?	*Spiller De (du) . . . ?*
May I join you?	*Må jeg være med?*
Would you like to join in?	*Vil De (du) være med?*
Would you like a game of . . . ?	*Skal vi spille . . . ?*
Well played!	*Godt spillet!*
Where is the swimming-pool?	*Hvor er simming-poolen?*
Can I hire a bathing costume and/or towel?	*Kan man leje badetøj og/eller håndklæde?*
Where are the tennis courts?	*Hvor er tennisbanerne?*
Is there a golf course?	*Er der en golfbane?*
Where can I fish?	*Hvor kan man fiske?*
I would like to water-ski	*Jeg vil gerne stå på vandski*
How much does it cost for a tow?	*Hvor meget koster båden der trækker?*
Can I have a motor boat?	*Kan man leje en motorbåd?*
I should like to hire a sailing boat	*Jeg vil gerne leje en sejlbåd*
Can I launch a boat here?	*Kan man sætte en båd i vandet her?*
Where can I moor?	*Hvor kan man lægge til?*
Can I hire the necessary equipment?	*Kan man leje det nødvendige udstyr?*
Where can I go horse riding?	*Hvor kan man ride?*
Where (when) can I see horse racing?	*Hvor (hvornår) kan man komme til hestevæddeløb?*
Where can I find a guide?	*Hvor kan man finde en guide?*
What is the weather forecast?	*Hvad lyder vejrudsigten på?*
I am only a beginner	*Jeg er kun begynder*
Where (when) can I see a football match?	*Hvor (hvornår) kan man komme til fodboldkamp?*
What is the score?	*Hvad er stillingen?*

athletics	*atletik*	bait	*madding, agn*
billiards	*billiard*	fishing reel	*fiskehjul*
boxing	*boksning*	fishing rod	*fiskestang*
bowls (game)	*bowling*	float	*svømmer*
cycling	*cykling*	hook	*krog*
darts	*pilespil*	landing net	*landingsnet*
football	*fodbold*	line	*snøre*
Fishing	**fiskeri**	spool	*spole*

Golf	**golf**
ball	*kugle*
bunker	*bunker*
caddie	*caddie*
golf club (place)	*golfklub*
(driver)	*golfkølle*
golf course	*golfbane*
green	*green*
hole	*hul*
miniature golf	*minigolf*
putt	*putt*
Horse Racing	**Hestevæddeløb**
bet	*indsats*
flat race	*fladløb*
grandstand	*tribune*
horse	*hest*
jockey	*jockey*
steeplechase	*terrænridning*
tote	*totalisator*
Horse Riding	**Ridning**
horse	*hest*
jump	*spring*
pony trekking	*pony trekking*
rein	*tømme*
ride	*ride*
saddle	*sadel*

stirrup	*stigbøjle*
Sailing	**Sejlsport**
anchor	*anker*
helm	*ror*
lifejacket	*redningsvest*
mast	*mast*
sails	*sejl*
Swimming	**Svømning**
bathing costume	*badedragt*
dive, to	*dykke, at*
swim, to	*svømme, at*
swimming-pool	*svømmebassin*
Tennis	**Tennis**
balls	*bolde*
doubles	*double*
partner	*medspiller*
racket	*ketsjer*
service	*serve*
singles	*single*
tennis court	*tennisbane*
Water Skiing	**Vandskisport**
motor boat	*motorbåd*
skis	*ski*
tow-rope	*slæbetov*
water ski, to	*at stå på vandski*

Tipping

Keep the change	*Jeg skal ikke have tilbage*
Tip	*Drikkepenge*

Travel

Train/Bus

Tog/bus

Can you help me with my luggage?	*Kan De (du) hjælpe mig med min bagage?*
I shall take this myself	*Den (det) her tager jeg selv*
Don't leave this	*Husk den (det) der*
Where is the . . . ?	*Hvor er . . . ?*
What is the fare to . . . ?	*Hvad koster billetten til . . . ?*
Give me a first- (second-) class ticket for . . .?	*Jeg vil gerne have en første- (anden-) klasses billet til . . . ?*
I want a sleeping berth	*Jeg vil gerne have en sovevogns-plads*
I want to reserve a seat	*Jeg vil gerne have en pladsbillet*
What time is the next (last) train for . . . ?	*Hvornår kører næste (sidste) tog til . . . ?*
From which platform (stop) does it leave?	*Hvilken perron kører det fra?*
Where is the booking (enquiry) office?	*Hvor er billetkontoret (oplyskingskontoret)?*
Do you stop at . . . ?	*Standser De ved . . . ?*
Must I change for . . . ?	*Skal jeg skifte undervejs . . .?*
Is this right for . . . ?	*Er det det rigtige tog (den rigtige bus) til . . . ?*
Where (when) are the meals served?	*Hvor (hvornår) serveres der mad?*
This seat is reserved	*Denne plads er reserveret*

Someone has taken my seat	*Der er nogen der har taget min plads*
Can you find me another seat?	*Kan De finde mig en anden plads?*
Is this seat vacant?	*Er denne plads optaget?*
This seat is (not) vacant	*Denne plads er (ikke) optaget*
May I open (close) the window?	*Må jeg åbne (lukke) vinduet?*
Where is the toilet?	*Hvor er toilettet?*
Where are we?	*Hvor er vi?*
I want to put my luggage in the left-luggage office	*Jeg vil gerne stille min bagage i garderoben*
How much do I owe you?	*Hvad koster det?*
Taxi hire	**Taxa**
Is there a taxi?	*Er der en taxa?*
I am going to . . .	*Jeg skal til . . .*
Here is the address	*Her er adressen*
I am in a hurry	*Jeg har travlt*
Will you drive as quickly as possible	*Vil De køre så hurtigt som muligt*
Go more slowly	*Kør lidt langsommere*

airline office	*luftfartskontor*	next (one)	*næste*
airport	*lufthavn*	next to	*ved siden af*
arrival	*ankomst*	number	*nummer*
bag	*taske*	passenger	*passager*
berth	*køje*	passport	*pas*
blanket	*tæppe*	pillow	*pude*
boat	*båd*	platform	*perron*
booking office	*billetkontor*	platform ticket	*perronbillet*
bus	*bus*	port	*havn* (harbour)
carriage (coach)	*vogn*	porter	*drager*
coach	*bus*	railway	*jernbane*
compartment	*kupe*	seat	*plads*
communication cord	*nødbremse*	seat reservation	*pladsbestilling*
connection	*forbindelse*	smoking compartment	*rygekupe*
Customs	*told*	station	*station*
Customs officer	*toldbetjent*	station master	*stationsforstander*
departure	*afgang*	stop	*stop*
dining-car	*spisevogn*	subway	*tunnel*
door	*dør*	suitcase	*kuffert*
driver	*fører*	taxi	*taxa*
entrance	*indgang*	ticket, single	*enkeltbillet*
exit	*udgang*	(return)	*(returbillet)*
fare	*billetpris*	tickets, book of	*billethæfte*
half-fare	*halv pris*	timetable	*fartplan*
inquiry office	*oplysningskontor*	train	*tog*
journey	*rejse*	tram	*sporvogn*
label	*mærke*	trunk	*stor kuffert*
last (adj)	*sidst*	waiting-room	*ventesal*
luggage	*bagage*	window	*vindue*
luggage-van	*bagagevogn*		